CELEBRATION

Book 1

Pentecost to All Saints
with Harvest and Remembrance

Edited by Brian Frost and Derek Wensley

Illustrated by Margaret Francis

GALLIARD LIMITED

Queen Anne's Road, Great Yarmouth, Norfolk

New York: Galaxy Music Corporation, 2121 Broadway,
New York, N.Y. 10020, U.S.A.

SBN 85249 090 9

ACKNOWLEDGEMENTS

It is believed all owners of copyright have been successfully traced and acknowledged and we are grateful for their ready co-operation, but if any rights have inadvertently been overlooked we apologise for this and will be pleased to acknowledge these in future editions.

Printed in Great Britain by Galliard Limited, Great Yarmouth, Norfolk, England.

BIRTHDAY (Pentecost or a Church Anniversary)

In this script, the designations used are C. Congregation, L. Leader of Worship, 1,2,3,4. Readers (who may if desired be replaced by a single reader or the leader). The script allows total involvement of the rest of the congregation without requiring them to take speaking parts. If used at Pentecost or at a church anniversary in summer, the elimination of as much daylight as possible will add to the effectiveness of the candles.

C. Song. You were there (*Faith, Folk & Festivity*) amending the first line of v. 6 to read "*I meet you God each Sunday*".

L. Ephesians 1.3–14 (*majestic music is played on organ or record at the end*).

1. There are two ways of looking at a birthday
Backwards
Or forwards

In the following narration if this is a Church Anniversary service then quote the appropriate number of years in place of 69.

2. You can either say
I'm 69 years old
Which is true;
Or 69 years young
Which for Christians
Promised an inheritance
In the perfecting of all creation.
A future rich beyond our imagining
Is most wonderfully true.

2. A birthday may be likened
To a tree in the glorious colours of the Autumn
Or to a plant edging through the soil of the Spring
Pushing upwards in faith and hope
Towards a mysterious tomorrow (*pause*)

3. There are two ways of looking at the birthday of God.
Backwards to a crib and a cross,
Two thousand years old;

4. Or forwards hands held by a risen Christ

3. Before us,

4. Within us,

3. Around us,

3 & 4. Who was from the beginning and shall be for ever
Ageless years young. (*pause*)

1. There are two ways of looking at the birthday of the church

2. Strange happenings noted by Luke
In his breath-taking reporting
Of the Acts of the Apostles:
Unlikely long-ago events
Hard to believe: can they be an example perhaps
From another age of sensational reporting? Maybe. Maybe not. (*pause*)

L. Acts 2.1–23, 32b–41 (*alternatively this may be spoken by a group of voices*)

The following lines should be spoken slowly, allowing time for listeners to catch the full wonder of the power of the Spirit.

2. This seems certain as you read behind the headlines.
Here is a mysterious power at work in the lives of men!
Providing them with a superhuman courage

Convincing them of their vital part in the perfecting of God's creation
Energised now to do more than any dared to ask or imagine,
Fired to the depth of their being by a present power,
Awesome in its intensity, blinding in its vision,
Strangely warm in its comfort, bewildering in its mystery

(*pause, with music on record or from organ*).

2.   To them in those pages of far-off history
1.   And not to us?
2.   Celebrating a requiem for the brave dead of the past?
1.   Or celebrating a mysterious yet certain partnership
With those fellow members of the Body of Christ from another age.
Left hand to their right. Right foot to their left.
1 & 2.   Equally co-partners in the perfecting of God's plan.
C.   Song. The day of the Spirit (*Faith, Folk & Festivity*).

The lights are dimmed to leave the church lit by candles, one on the communion table or altar and one at each door and window. A group of worshippers, each carrying lighted candles, process slowly into the church.

3.   There are two ways of looking at (a) the birthday of this church. (*Use "a" at Pentecost or "the" at a church anniversary*.)
4.   See the birthday candles
Carried in procession
In thanksgiving;
Each light a symbol of partnership with Christians of an earlier age
Who, like us, sometimes more, sometimes less faithfully
Have allowed the light of God to shine on them,
In them, through them, from them;
3.   Or you can see the procession of candles
Lighting, each one but dimly,
Yet powerfully together, a forward road.

The worshippers disperse about the church each to his separate pew.

3.   But wait, they separate.
Strange! I thought they would each have placed
Their separate candles together by the table of the Lord
That we together might discern the way ahead.
4.   But no! each has gone to his separate seat,
Placed his light upon the ground
That he may the more easily see the words in the book
As he kneels to pray.
Each by his own little light groping after God.
1.   Yet, what are these other lights?
Candles of brightness not held by human hands,
One by that door, one by this
One at each window,
2.   At each opening to the world—a candle!

As music plays the candles by windows and door are snuffed out.

3.   There was a time when each of these candles was unlit. When a solitary light on the table pierced the darkness all round. (*pause*)

During the following narration, another group of worshippers enters, most with candles burning brightly, one with candle nearly out. They follow the narrator's words.

4.   And there came in those days, when the church was ageless years young, a group of Christians carrying the Spirit of God within them. Men and women of many gifts they

were. Didn't all get on very well with each other. But they were knit together by a common purpose. Many times they came. Sometimes the light that one carried burned fiercely while another almost flickered out.

3.   But as they grouped themselves round the table of the Lord, the lights showed prominent against the shadows, the hand of one, the smile of another, the listening ear of the third, the watchful eyes of a fourth. One was carrying the tools of his trade, another the books of his profession, a doctor's bag, a baby's shawl, a violin . . .

4.   They passed round the bread and broke it and ate; they passed round the cup of wine and drank together, they looked to the one whose candle was almost out to see how they might share his burden, ready to do for him whatever would help, however menial, just as Jesus had once washed the tired feet of his friends. And each taking the other's hands, they wished each other peace and sent each other forth in hope in the name of the host of their table, Christ Jesus the Lord.

3.   They went their separate ways from the church, some to what the world calls high office, some to what the world calls the trivial round. They went, their light going with them. But as they went, they lit other lights as candles may. And they lit, as they passed by, lights in each window and at each door of the church for late travellers to see. They lit lights in commerce and industry, politics and education, home and hospital, hotel and hostel . . .

The second group of worshippers leave the church.

1.   Till one day, as they were all about God's business in God's world, a lost traveller who had been attracted to the church by the light of the candles took refuge there from a blustering gale; and carelessly, or accidentally, or on purpose—who can tell?—knocked over a candle till, in the twinkling of an eye the little light glowed ever more powerfully till it lit the whole countryside in flaming fire. It was as if, in making itself available to one need, the light blazed up with the power of a fiery furnace.

The church is for a moment full of light and then, save for the lights on the floor in the pews, every candle is extinguished. After a pause a single worshipper enters bearing his candle.

2.   One of the Christians, seeing the blaze, ran to the church he loved, to find the traveller stupified in the ruins of his beloved sanctuary. The building had stood ready to meet the human need of that traveller at the cost of its very life.

The rest of the worshippers return during the next narrative. The communion table becomes "John's table" in the action.

1.   There were two items on the agenda when the Christians met in John's house. Home for Christians? And home for a traveller? John placed the candle on the table and pressed close together in John's small room, they passed round the bread and broke and ate, and they passed round the cup of wine and drank together. And though he didn't understand what it was all about, the traveller too ate some bread and drank from the cup.

The group remain in a tableau round the communion table.

3.   No—this is not a story from the past of this local church!

4.   And yet, in a sense, is it?

1.   It is not a story from the future of this local church!

2.   And yet, might it be?

3.   And it is not a story of the present birthday of this local church (this Whitsuntide here in this church)!

4.   Is it a story for it? (*pause*)

1.   For you, 69 years young, a plant edging through the soil of the spring, pushing upwards in faith and hope towards an unknown tomorrow, going forward hands held by the risen Christ who was from the beginning and shall be for ever ageless years young, a procession of candles now dim, as each by his own light gropes after God: come, gather with these others yet round the table of the Lord (*they begin to move from their*

pews, candles held high—if desired, the stewards offer candles to each other person present), and let the Light of the host shine on your agenda paper. Home for travellers? Home for Christians? Birthday plans for the future made in the power of the spirit with you. For as you cling on to your buildings, your possessions, your souls, for yourselves, they will be of no consequence: but as the Spirit compels you to use them regardless of losing them, they shall be lights which no man can put out.

The bread is passed hand to hand; and the cup also, each shakes hands with another and speaks "Peace".

L.   Home for travellers? Home for Christians? Let us work out what shall be done.

The Leader of worship carries his light with the others following till the church is empty but for one solitary candle burning on the table of the Lord: the Christians in groups in a hall, in homes as may be best continue to study the agenda. If a choir is available, they should sing "Thou mastering me" (Faith, Folk & Festivity) as they process behind the others to leave the church.
Either later that day or on a separate occasion, the congregation should reassemble for the following short act of worship.

C.   *(sing or read corporately)* Te Deum
L.   Ephesians 1.3–14.
C.   Fire is lighting torch and lamp at night *(Faith, Folk & Festivity)*.
1, 2, 3, 4. Acts 11.1–18 *(read by several voices)*.
C.   Hymn. The Trinity of Mutual Love *(Faith, Folk & Festivity)*.

Spokesmen for the groups who had met for discussion or a spokesman for all of them speaks a series of sentences.

We commend that this church seeks in the power of the Spirit to . . . *(here follows the recommendations for action each followed by a period of silence long enough to think on the significance of the proposal).*

C.   Hymn. O Church of God arise *(Annie Matheson)* *(to be found in most hymnbooks including Methodist Hymn Book No. 795)* or Lord of the Dance *(Sydney Carter)* *(Faith, Folk & Clarity or Faith, Folk & Nativity)* or I bind unto myself today *(St Patrick)*.

L.   John 15.4, 5, 7, 8.
C.   Thanks be to God.
L.   Ephesians 3.20–21.

Congregational Sheet

BIRTHDAY

Song. You were there *(see Note A)*
Reading. Ephesians 1.3–14
"There are two ways of looking at a birthday . . ."
Reading. Acts 2.1–23, 32b–41
". . . Read behind the headlings . . ."
Song. The day of the spirit *(see Note A)*
"There are two ways of looking at (a) the birthday of this church"
(Use "a" if the script is used at Pentecost or "the" if at a church anniversary)
Sequence around "John's table"
Group discussion

———

Te Deum
Reading. Ephesians 1.3-14
Hymn. Fire is lighting torch and lamp at night *(see Note A)*
Reading. Acts 11.1–18
Hymn. The Trinity of mutual love *(see Note B)*

"We commend that this church seeks in the power of the spirit, to . . ."
Hymn (enter choice) (*if "Lord of the Dance" is chosen, see Note A*)
Reading. St John 15.4–5, 7–8 (*after which the congregation say "Thanks be to God"*)
Dismissal. Ephesians 3.20–21
Note A: *If it is desired to duplicate copyright words of these songs for use by the congregation, permission can be granted on payment of a fee of 50p (10/–) for each song to Galliard Ltd, Queen Anne's Road, Great Yarmouth, Norfolk*
Note B: *If it is desired to duplicate copyright words of this hymn application should be made to Society of the Sacred Mission, Kelham, Notts*

THE GIFT OF LANGUAGE (Pentecost)

*The congregation is, by use of contemporary theatrical techniques reduced to speechlessness
and rescued therefrom.*

*If possible, seat the congregation in the round. Locate seven "voices" throughout the congrega-
tion, one in the pulpit and another at an entrance door.*

*The priest and deacon enter without prelude, and take arbitrary standing positions, orientated
neither to the table, the building, the congregation nor each other. As they enter, service folders are
hurriedly distributed so that the congregation has no advance notice of what they are expected to
say. The techniques used mean that the service should not be repeated amongst the same group of
people.*

*In this script: C = Congregation, D = Deacon, L = Priest (Leader of Worship), VS = Voices,
V2S = Voices in two groups, P = Voice at door, E = Voice at Entrance, 1, 2, 3, 4, 5, 6, 7 =
Voices in Congregation.*

*In the first part of the script, the Liturgy is printed in bold type and the language printed on the
congregational sheet is printed in bold capitals.*

OPENING LITURGY

L.   **Let us pray** (*silence is allowed to grow embarrassing*).

L.   **WE CONFESS.**

C.   **THAT EVENTS WILL GO ON AND ON.**

VS   (*from one to another in circle round room continuing through next two speeches*). And on,
     and on, and on . . .

1.   But you can't confess what's going to happen.

2.   What else should we confess? About what has happened we can do nothing (*pause*).

L.   **WE PRAY.**

C.   **THAT WE HAVE SINNED AGAINST THEE BY OUR FAULT.**

VS   (*as before*). Our fault, our fault . . .

1.   But you can't pray for the past.

2.   But what should we pray for the future?

V2S (*through following liturgy*). We pray, we pray . . . *or* We confess, we confess . . .

L.   **We will say what we can. WE CONFESS.**

C.   **THAT WE HAVE SPENT A VERY LONG TIME EVOLVING.**

L.   **OUR SIN IS GREAT.**

C.   **OUR OXYGEN AND HYDROGEN ARE WICKEDLY PAIRED.**

3.   With whom are we paired?

P.   Tomorrow will be better. Tomorrow she will be what I did not know.

L.   **WE PRAY** and/or confess.

C.   **OUR SIM-ULTANEOUS TRANSLATIONS BEGIN AND END EXACTLY ON
     TIME, THOUGH THE ORIGINAL IS OFTEN OBSCURE. OUR SIN AND COSINE
     ARE EFFICIENT: OUR SIN-ECURES ARE SIN-CERELY SCIN-TILLATING.
     OUR SIN IS GREAT.**

V2S (*spoken during previous congregational passage*). We are what we are what we are what . . .
     or We will be what we will be what we . . . (*obliterating crash of dischord on organ ends
     dialogue*) (*pause*)

The following is expressionless. Flat.

D.   What is the trouble? Why cannot we speak?

P.   You can. You are speaking now.

D.   That is only dramatic convention. I repeat: why cannot we speak?

4.   Because your past has no future and your future no past (*pause*).

5.   What is there to talk about?

D.   What has been. We have tried and failed to speak thereof. Why cannot we say what has
     been?

5. About what you have been there is nothing to say that can make any difference—except what it means for what you will be.
D. Then we should speak of the future. But we have failed in this also. Why cannot we say what we will be?
6. Find a past that has a future. And find a future that can be told, as can be told, as can the past.
D. What?
7. Find a past tale you can also await as your future. Have a tale of past love to tell as future hope.
D. What?
1. Get someone who you know has loved you to live as your goal in the future.
D. What?
2. Get someone to rise from the dead (*organ dischord ends dialogue*). *Nothing happens. Silence is held for at least five minutes.*

PRAYERS
L. **LET US PRAY.**
   For all good things of whatsoever sort, and in confidence in thy revelatory arms, by which we daily increase in saving longing for all good things of whatsoever.
C. **LORD HAVE MERCY.**
L. **For thy peace which passes politics, in so far of course as is compatible with thy blessings to us as a people.**
C. **LORD HAVE MERCY.**
VS (*from one to another in circle round room*). Lord, have tuppence.
L. **For thy word. Almighty Spirit of one that is above all change and decay to which we are fallen.**
C. **LORD HAVE MERCY.**
VS (*as before*). Lord, have at you.
   Organ dischords begin softly, crescend slowly through following.
L. **By our grievous sin from which if we only repent Lord enough at thy Word, Almighty Spirit of one that is above.**
3. Why cannot we speak?
C. **LORD HAVE MERCY.**
VS (*as before*). Sssshhhh.
L. **All change and decay to which we are fallen by.**
4. Why cannot we speak?
C. **LORD HAVE MERCY.**
VS (*as before*). Sssshhhh.
   By now the organ is so loud nothing can be heard.
E. (*in loud but expressionless shout, repeated until audible over organ, whereupon organ stops*). He is risen! He is risen! (*pause*). Say it! (*pause*). Say something! (*pause*). Say "I" (*pause*). You can do it for he who was, whose story you know, will love you again. You have, therefore, a past self and a future self that cohere. You can say "I".
VS I.
E. You can all say "I".
VS (*repeated until congregation join in*). I.
C. I.
E. He is risen! (*pause*). You can say "I believe" (*pause*). It doesn't matter whether you think you do or not. He knows your past and will one day tell you about it. And then he will be your future. So you can take the risk of affirming what you have been and will be. You can believe in something. Say "I believe".
VS (*repeated until congregation join in*). I believe.
E. And here is something worth talking about. Say "I believe in Jesus who was crucified and rose. He is risen." You can say it.
VS (*repeated until congregation join in*). I believe in Jesus who was crucified and rose.
E. Good. Here is shorthand for all that (*pause*). You can say "God".
VS and C. God.

At utterance of "God" the clergy snap out of their frozen positions and take appropriate clergy seating. The liturgy now continues without interruption from voices.

LESSONS. *Acts 2.1–11 and John 14.23–31. These are read, without sentences or interspersed singing, and preferably by readers from their places in the congregation.*

SERMON.

OFFERTORY: *The table is set, the gifts of money and the bread and wine placed on it, and the vessels prepared for the meal.*

A PRAYER of the church is said by the leader with petitions and intercessions for the occasions, referring always to the gift of language and of a gospel to be said. As in Contemporary Prayers for Public Worship, p. 53 No. 17 and p. 44 No. 2. To each petition, the congregation responds: **WE BESEECH THEE TO HEAR US, GOOD LORD.**

THE THANKSGIVING
Preface (*congregation rises*) and Sanctus (*spoken*).
Prayer of Thanksgiving (*congregation kneels*) as in Lutheran Service Book (*any good Eucharistic prayer will be equally suitable*) (*or as in Contemporary Prayers for Public Worship, p. 88 No. 3, with the Our Father spoken*).
Communion. *As each group gathers around the table, they greet each other in peace—the celebrant greets the first communicant with a handshake and the greeting* **THE PEACE OF THE LORD BE WITH YOU,** *and he, the one next to him, and so on through the group. During the Communion, the choir sings a hymn of thanksgiving, e.g. "Now thank we all our God" (this is the first music in the service).*
Post-Communion
L. We have not only heard, we have seen, touched and tasted. We cannot only speak, we can sing. We can all sing. Hymn No. ....
A congregational hymn is sung, e.g. "Come down, O Love Divine".
Benediction
Festal Recession with music.

Congregational Sheet
THE GIFT OF LANGUAGE (Pentecost)

OPENING LITURGY
L. We confess
C. That events will go on and on
L. We pray
C. That we have sinned against thee by our own fault
L. We confess
C. That we have spent a very long time evolving
L. Our sin is great
C. Our oxygen and hydrogen are wickedly paired
L. We pray
C. Our sim-ultaneous translations begin and end exactly on time, though the original is often obscure. Our sin and cosine are efficient. Our sin-ecures are sin-cerely scin-tillating. Our sin is great

PRAYERS
L. Let us pray
    (*Petitions.*)
C. (*after each petition*). Lord, have mercy

LESSONS

SERMON

OFFERTORY
Offering of bread, wine and money
Prayer (*congregation kneels*)
L.   (*each petition*)
C.   We beseech thee to hear us, good Lord

THE THANKSGIVING
The Preface (*congregation rises*)
Prayer of Thanksgiving (*congregation kneels*)
L.   Holy art thou . . . but deliver us from evil
C.   For thine is the Kingdom, and the power, and the glory for ever and ever. Amen
The Communion: *As each group gathers around the table, they greet each other in peace. The celebrant will greet one communicant with a handshake and the greeting* "The peace of the Lord be with you" *and he, the one next to him, and so on through the group*
Post-Communion

REFLECTIONS FOR TRINITY SUNDAY

The following designations are used: L = Leader of Worship, 1,2,3,4 = Readers.

L. Let us pray for understanding of God and our relationship with him. Lord God, our Father, Son and Holy Spirit, help us to understand you and come close to you. We have come together to discover what you are. Perhaps we will be surprised at what we find. But then we are always being surprised about you, because you are greater than we had ever imagined, and capable of such love that death has no power to destroy it.
God the Father, help us to understand what your fatherhood means: God the Son, show us the way you trod and make us fit to be your brothers; God the Holy Spirit, set us free from everything that hinders our worship, and lead us forward into new dimensions of truth. Amen.

GOD THE FATHER

C. Hymn *on the Fatherhood of God, possibly "Praise, my soul, the King of Heaven".*
L. Our hope in God is firmly based on his promises to us as Father, as Son, as Holy Spirit. But what can this mean for us today? Listen to the promise of Fatherhood and see what sense it makes.
1. Romans 8.14–17.
L. What did you make of your father? What sort of a father was he? Was he strong, domineering, authoritarian, weak and passive or strong and demanding. How did you react to him? What do you make of him now? Does his hidden presence still rule you however much you try to deny it—or have you thought you've forgotten him only to find his power still holds you in thrall?

Two members of the congregation are interviewed on the spot asking them what they recall of their fathers.

L. We've heard from our friends what they think about this. And we have been made to think about our own fathers. But perhaps we can see most dramatically what people think about fathers by looking at the student revolt—for here we can see the idea of fatherhood in a society being overturned by student power.
Are they rebelling because they are difficult young people? Are they over-reacting to their own upbringing or are students pointing to something which has gone wrong with fatherhood—it has become authoritarian because it can no longer speak with authority, it has become oppressive because it has become moralistic.
The psychologist Sigmund Freud was the great prophet who made us look at ourselves and the society we live in and ask what kind of father we wanted and allowed. Do we make a God in our own image—or a society? Because we are anxious and insecure, do we make God able to protect us; because we feel the need for ethics for our society, do we create a standard for them from a God of our devising? And then impose this view on other people?
Our Bible reading tells us that there is a freedom for us in the God of Christ. He enables us to be ourselves over against him. But there is a price to pay—God our Father allows us suffering and pain. He is not over-protective or domineering. We can reject Him because we are free. We can suffer because we are human and have responsibility for our own lives.

GOD THE SON

C. Hymn *on the sonship of Jesus Christ, possibly "Son of God, Eternal Saviour".*
L. Our hope in God is built on promise—promise not only of fatherhood, but of sonship also. Listen to the promise of sonship and see what sense it makes.
2. Galatians 3.26–28.
L. What did you make of your son?
What did your parents make of making a son of you?

Were they weak—or strong?
Was your son over-obedient?
Or perhaps compliant? Conformist?
Was a relationship established between you—or stony silence?
Do you still work out the effects of this today in your own life?

Two members of the congregation are interviewed on the spot asking them what they recall of their sons—or their experience of being a son (or daughter).

L. We've heard what our friends think about this. And I expect we've been made to think about our own relationships. But again just as we did when we thought about our experience of fatherhood—either personally, or in our society—we can see sonship in its different forms by looking at something outside ourselves.

For just as there are fathers and fathers, so there are sons and sons. A good son, maybe one who never asserts himself, is always thought of as "good". A bad son is not necessarily "bad". We can put people in rôles too easily.

The American theologian Harvey Cox has written an interesting essay on sloth. In his book "On not leaving it to the snake" he says he thinks the awful sin the Bible speaks of in the Garden of Eden was sloth. Here was man pictured in the garden given all the good things of the earth by God yet he didn't want to use his powers and his responsibilities properly. He didn't want to grow up. He wanted a God who would run the show for him.

It wasn't sex or wanting to be like God which was the point of the garden story: it was man's failure to come to terms with his power and his capacity. He was always wanting to run in the other direction. To deny his sonship in fact—to deny his capacity for satisfying relationships because the task was too difficult. In our reading from the Bible there was a lot of talk about "in Christ" there is nothing of the normal kind of distinctions we make—Communist and Christian, Jew and Arab, Russian and American.

How that view threatens our security systems! How it attacks the barriers we have carefully built up around us to protect ourselves from the demands, claims of others—how that nicely checks our growth into mature relationships! You can see this sloth everywhere—in your home, in your street, the places where you work, the trade unions, the factory canteen, the office and the company, and in the world of international relationships.

Sigmund Freud used to explore the problems of people trying to come to a real maturity. He saw them as the problem of helping the healthy ego to come to fruition. But he saw what he called the super-ego—the part of ourselves still dominated by the demands of the past experience of our parents on us. This super-ego stunts our growth and curbs our true welfare. Our childhood had not yet broken into mature humanity. We are not willing to be independent, to take responsibility, for we still want an outside authority to solve everything for us.

So too with the Christian sonship. Jesus makes no attempt to get the rich young ruler to give up his wealth. He did not try to dissuade Judas from betraying him. He expected his disciples to draw the right conclusions for themselves. "Have I been so long time with you, and does thou not know me, Philip?" They must stand on their own feet as he stood on his. This was the great difference between Him and the Pharisees, even between his disciples and the disciples of John the Baptist. Jesus' disciples were not his servants but his friends. In the same way they were not God's slaves, they are sons, with all the liberty of a son.

God the Holy Spirit

C. Hymn on the Holy Spirit, *possibly "The Spirit of the Lord revealed".*

3. John 14.15–18.

L. What are we to make of the work of the Spirit?

What are we to make of this promise? We can begin to understand the work of the Father, we can see, because we have a picture of Jesus, the work of Christ, but what of the spirit?

Perhaps we catch a glimpse of it in this passage. Because we are given an indication of hate.

Hate? How can that be? Jesus said the result of being called his friends would bring hatred. That there is an essential tension to be found where he is at work. This tension will bring out hate as well as love. And we are to expect that.

The work of the spirit is the work of tension—of allowing the possibility of brokenness in relationships: but it is a creative tension which implies a unity as well as a discontinuity.

I wonder if any of you feel you can talk about experiences you may have had involving great tension, where nevertheless there was creativity.

Two or three members of the congregation are interviewed in the hope of drawing out this point from the experience of the people present.

L.   There is obviously a difference between a destructive and a creative tension. In a group you can often have more life when there is a creative tension, when there are members who disagree violently with each other than a group which tries to pretend this does not exist and successfully kills off those who disagree by ignoring them.

Man's work, too, must provide the possibility of a creative tension between him and other people and between him and his environment. Take man's work from him and something important to his rôle, his stature and his meaning goes. For man does not work for bread alone: he works for meaning, for creativity.

But obviously there are spirits and spirits. What is a good spirit and a bad spirit? How can we judge one from another, be discriminating in our assessment of the work of the spirit?

Some people feel it is right to fight an oppressor, others not to drop bombs. For some British policy on the Middle East and Rhodesia, or America's on Viet Nam is wicked; for others inevitable, given the nuances of politics.

Obviously there can be no blueprint—but we have been given guidelines. His voice is heard where there are tensions, where people fight exploitation and tyranny, where people proclaim and fight for freedom, where people proclaim and work through conflict to reconciliation.

Member of congregation stands up from back with "prearranged spontaneity"

4.   I don't know about all the others here. This is all very interesting. But I'm puzzled. You see what puzzles me is how can there be three experiences of God—How can God be Father, Son and Spirit together? Is God divided, or is he the same person? That's the point I'd like to see resolved. And I'd like to believe it made any difference to me anyway.

L.   I think there is a way of doing this. I've asked three people to act out this rôle play for you. They each know Mr X—but from three very different points of view. (*Here ensues a rôle play where three people sit around a table and discuss Mr X—they decide who it is to be—it can be a known or an unknown person. The essential point is that each person round the table knows only one facet of the person discussed and knows nothing of the other. The surprise each finds in knowing the other two parts can be imagined. The rôle play should be allowed to go on for as long as necessary to make the point powerfully, but not too long to bore.*)

L.   Three people, yet one person. And I imagine if you went to the mother of that person she would say—yes, they are all my son (or daughter). They are each part but only part of the whole who remains a mystery, more than the sum of those three parts.

So with God—we experience Him in three ways, but he is always more than that—he is always the mystery who offers us a promise. He is: he has shown us in our experience, in the life of the church and its tradition, and in our own lives in the world, an intimation of what he is like. But he is always egging us on to greater heights—to a greater experience if you like! To a less distorted picture of the father: To mature understanding of sonship: To more ability to live with creative tensions, where we come through to interdependence with other people and other nations and where we learn to be stewards as fathers over his creation. Without any one of these living experiences we are less than human. When we think we have got it all taped we have lost the mystery—of ourselves and of God.

The response

L. So we make our response in prayer, first in confession.

1. God, we acknowledge you as Father, completely to be trusted, loving each one of us as your child. But we have ignored you. If we hadn't, then the world would show the marks of your fatherhood. Forgive us for turning the good things you have given us into objects which tyrannise us. Forgive us for not sharing the wealth of the world properly. We want to say that we too have played a part in bringing about this suffering world, we your sons.

2. God, we know you as Son, as one who shared in the dust and joy of human existence. You tried to show us what it is to be a son of God, taking responsibility. But we ignore you. We are not all brothers, not even those who have the nerve to use your name. We are suspicious of each other, because we all think we are right and don't need others to help us. Forgive us our failure to love as your mature sons. And make us brave for the future.

3. God, you live in us as Holy Spirit, bringing out our capacity for tension. We know how we have evaded your stirrings within us. We have not let you lead us into action for what is right and just: we have preferred to follow our own insights and have abused our freedom. We haven't been willing to work for reconciliation and freedom. We confess we have an artificial peace with each other; we are not really free. So how can we go forward?

L. A prayer of pardon (*from Contemporary Prayers for Public Worship p. 42 No 1*). As a mark of our desire to live the new life to which God calls us, and through a real desire to experience his fullness, we pray:

Prayers of Intercession (*these should be prepared by three or four members of the congregation, linking up Fatherhood, Sonship and the Spirit's work in experience in the world. They should include topics of current concern to the congregation*).

The offering is received.

Prayer of Dedication (*said by all*).
    O God, source of all light
    In whom is perfect group life,
    We offer to you the group life
    Of the world:
        in our families,
        in our streets,
        in our neighbourhoods, towns and boroughs.
    We ask you to empower
    The groups of men in nations
    Seeking a united world.
    Give to all groups
    The courage to face their problems—
    And possibilities—
    Their constructive hate
    And their destructive love.

    Enable the group life of the world
    To tolerate conflict,
    Intensify dialogue
    And live in the glory
    Of the undivided power of your life
    Where all men are one.

C. Hymn *on The Trinity, possibly "Thou, whose almighty word"*.

L. The Blessing.

REFLECTIONS FOR TRINITY SUNDAY

"We worship one God in Trinity, and Trinity in Unity . . . the Father incomprehensible, the Son incomprehensible, and the Holy Ghost incomprehensible . . . there are not three incomprehensibles but one incomprehensible . . . He therefore that will be saved must thus think of the Trinity."—Extracts from the Creed of St Athanasius

Prayer for understanding

God the Father
Hymn
Reading. Romans 8.15–17
Reflections on "Father"

God the Son
Hymn
Reading. Galatians 3.26–28
Reflections on "Son"

God the Holy Spirit
Hymn
Reading. John 14.15–18
Reflections on "Tension"
What's the point of "Trinity"?

The Response
Prayers of Confession
Prayer of Pardon
Prayers of Intercession
The Offering
Prayer of Dedication said by all (*type out from main script*)
Hymn

The Blessing

BENEDICITE (Harvest)

The author assumed this would be used on a family occasion and for that reason the Noah section has been included. Ordinary lighting is assumed which allows presentation in daylight. The original choice of hymns is given, contemporary songs have been indicated as alternatives. The congregation is designated C. Readers designated 1,2,3, in the script might be in the pulpit, at the lectern and in the centre aisle. When these readers speak together, the designation G is shown. Children are designated as follows: A = a single child, B = chorus of children (spoken). D = chorus of children (spoken), E = choir of children (alternatively spoken). The song "One more river" is found in many collections of negro songs including "Oxford Song Book, Vol 2" (Oxford University Press). The actual words of the Benedicite at the beginning of each section may be spoken or sung by the voices shown.

C.   HYMN. To thee, O Lord, our hearts *or* SONG. Creation's song. (*Faith, Folk & Festivity*)

> *Short extract of Music (light orchestral/pastoral) followed by silence. A gong sounds once.*

1.   Benedicite
2.   Benedicite omnia opera.
3.   O all ye works of the Lord, bless ye the Lord,
G.   Praise him and magnify him for ever
1.   This is a song of creation
And of creation's delight
In its creator.
We are part of that creation
And we should rejoice in it,
We should be able to sing
With the stars and the winds,
With the dews and the frosts.
But our hearts are heavy
And our tongues are tied.
We are no longer children,
The springtime is over,
The days are dying,
The lights are fading
And we have no home.
We have wandered the world,
We have climbed the mountains
And tunnelled in the earth.
We have searched the scriptures
And listened to the wise,
And yet we remain
The lost delinquents
Of the Eternal.
2.   This is man's adolescence.
No longer child
With only brief intimations
Of responsible maturity.
Too proud to worship,
Too clever to believe,
Too exalted to seek forgiveness,
Too high minded
In a low minded way.

3.   We have mastered our dimensions,
      We have analysed the earth,
      We have perfected our artificials,
      We have pursued every grub and insect,
      Every weed and wild flower
      With our carefully selected selectives.
      We are the masters,
      To us surely is the power and the glory.
      We are the reapers and sowers,
      We have made our magnificent machines.
      To master the harvest,
      To sow and reap,
      To bind and store,
      To dry and keep.
      We are the breadwinners of creation,
      We are the lords of all the earth. (*soft orchestral music*)
1.   But can we untangle the constellations?
      Can we delicately balance Pleiades?
      Or give orders to Orion?
      Or hobble Taurus?
      Or caution Cassiopeia?
2.   Can we light sister Sun,
      Or burnish brother Moon?
      Can we operate the thermostats
      Of Autumn, Winter, Summer, Spring?
3.   Can we manufacture the life germ
      In cabbage and cauliflower,
      In wheat and barley,
      In brussel sprout
      And rumbling radish?
3.   Yet we must sow
      And we must reap
      If we would eat.
2.   When the world was young
      Men sang Benedicite.
      Their song echoed, they believed,
      In the vaulted rafters
      Of the courts of heaven.
      Caught up and amplified
      By the endless praise
      Of angels and archangels
      Delighting the Eternal God
      And they delighting in him.
      And childlike
      They brought their harvest gifts
      As if to say,
      Lord, look how clever we have been
      Look how wisely we have used
      Your earth and rain and sun and sky,
      Lord most high.

C.   HYMN. All creatures of our God and King *or* SONG. Wonderful is Thy Handiwork.
      (*Faith, Folk & Festivity*)

1.   O ye powers of the Lord, bless ye the Lord,
2.   O ye children of men, bless ye the Lord,
3.   O ye priests of the Lord, bless ye the Lord,

1.   O ye servants of the Lord, bless ye the Lord.
2.   What is man that thou art mindful of him?
3.   When you come home in the evening
     And snugly stable the car,
     When you've eaten your fill
     And packed your pipe
     And tucked yourself in for television,
     Drooping soon in your armchair
     From an overdose of old movies,
     Or from seeing the same clue,
     Or hearing the same cliche
     For the 10th, 20th or 30th time;
     You relieve your infuriated tension
     By stretching for your whisky and water
     Or perhaps for your Benger's and biscuit.
     In an uncomfortable way you are comfortable,
     Not concerned about this or that
     Feeling quite certain
     That you've earned
     Your lack-lustre leisure
     And that you are doing yourself good
     In spite of your irritated droopings.
1.   Are you the crowning glory
     Of the long evolutionary processes?
     Is it for this life stirred
     In the primeval slimes?
     And that God rested
     After his six hard days
     Of creating heaven and earth?
2.   I have my books,
     I play my golf,
     I have salted away
     My savings
     In banks and unit trusts.
     I am insured against
     Rain and fire, torrent and terror.
     I have taken so many precautions
     That I am now sick with caution,
     So cautious that I dare not die.
3.   Lost in the labyrinths
     Of marvellous mechanisation
     With a sinking heart
     And a drooping spirit
     And a mind fearful,
     The lost fruit
     Of the world's harvest.
2.   I sit in my chair in the evening
     And in the brief silences
     I wonder about life and death,
     About birth and being.
     In my lazy half-hearted way
     I try to see the sense of it.
     To you it looks as if
     I am lazing away my leisure
     And you would ask your question
     "Are you the crowning glory

Of the long evolutionary processes?"
And I would answer "Yes, I am"
Take me or leave me,
Ridicule or torture me,
Curse me or kill me,
I am what it is all about.
I look from my swaying house
Of bones and muscles,
Of flesh sanctified by blood,
I search the skies
And cultivate the earth.
I know that I am not alone,
I have intimate fellowship
With mists and mountains
With beasts and birds and trees.
I from the depths of my
Television chair still try to sing
Benedicite.

1.   O ye works of men, bless ye the Lord
2.   O ye mechanical devices, bless ye the Lord
3.   O warm, well-fed, insurance-covered man, bless ye the Lord
     Praise him and magnify him forever.

C.   HYMN. O praise ye the Lord, praise Him in the height *or* SONG. Let the Cosmos Ring.
     (*Faith, Folk & Festivity*)

1.   O ye whales, bless ye the Lord.
2.   O ye fowls of the air, bless ye the Lord
3.   O ye beasts and cattle, bless ye the Lord.
G.   Praise him and magnify him for ever.
1.   God made the world
     And loved the world
     And generously lavished this love
     On all created things.
     Light and colour,
     Colour massed,
     Colour gently shading,
     Reds and blues,
     Greens and yellows,
     Fusing together subtly.
     Shades subduing
     And light intensifying
     The colour climate of creation.
2.   Singing and laughter,
     Rhythm and syncopation,
     The dancing delight
     Of the happy heart
     Echoing the ten thousand songs
     Of creation.
3.   And God said "Let the earth bring forth the living
     creature after his kind, cattle and creeping thing,
     the beasts of the earth after his kind", and it was so.
2.   He made them long and tall and fair,
     He made them round and fat and stubby,
     He made some gentle and some fierce
     And some were mean and short and grubby.
1.   God made great beasts,

            God made great whales
            and winged fowls,
            Cattle and creeping things.
    3.   But the ancient story tells
            of tempter, serpent, devil,
            Corrupting creation.
            And it made the Lord God angry
            When he saw all the wickedness
            That was great upon the face of the earth.
    1.   And God said, I will destroy it all
            And start all over again.
    2.   He decided to rip open
            The firmament of heaven
            And to cause the deep wells
            To burst forth
            And to make floods dark and deep
            On the face of the earth.
    3.   For the Lord was sorry that he had made it all.
            But he loved faithful Noah
            And all his ingenious animals.
    1.   He loved the animals
            The fishes and the birds
            That he had given to man
            For his pleasure
            And for his food.
    2.   God loved the patient animals,
            He loved the roaring beasts.
            God saw them all
            And thought them very good.
    3.   And he ordered his servant Noah
            To make a great ship
            And to store in it
            Seed and grain,
            Birds and beasts,
            Sons and daughters,
            So that he might think again
            And replenish the earth.
    E.   Old Noah he did build the ark
            There's one more river to cross
            He patched it up with hickory bark
            There's one more river to cross
            There's one more river
            And that's the river of Jordan
            There's one more river
            There's one more river to cross.
    1.   And Noah and Shem
            And Ham and Japheth
            And Mrs Noah and Mrs Shem
            And Mrs Ham and Mrs Japheth
            Organised the animals
            Into long, long lines
            And told them to be on their best behaviour
            And keep still
            To be ready
            To run and hop and skip
            Up the gang planks

24

When the rain began
And the waters started to rise.

E. The animals went in one by one
The elephant chewing a caraway bun.

2. And when the weather forecast said
Rain and more rain,
Rain for ever and ever
Stormy conditions
And fearful floods
In many places.
The animals speeded up.

E. The animals went in two by two
The rhinoceros and the kangaroo. (*pause*)

E. The animals went in four by four
The great hippopotamus stuck in the door. (*pause*)

E. The animals went in six by six
The hyena laughed at the monkey's tricks,
There's one more river.
And that's the river of Jordan
There's one more river
One more river to cross.

3. So when we come to
Harvest home,
Remember your friends,
The animals
That suffer so much
And bear so much
That men like us
Might live.

2. Without them you would not have made it.
You would have never survived
The dangerous paths
Of dubious evolution
If they had not been there
To feed and sustain you,
If they had not
Carried your burdens
And drawn your ploughs.

3. But we don't need them now
We are mechanised
And with our Massey Fergusons
We can plough and reap and sow.

1. But still the earth needs to be loved
And the animals to be cared for.
Don't let the tractors
Turn our hearts into pumps,
Don't let the machines
Mechanise our minds
We take our place in creation
With the fish and the beasts and the birds.

2. And God gave us dominion
That we might enjoy and not destroy.
That we might explore creation's limits.
O God how wonderful are Thy works,
Thy glory shall endure for ever.

E. *quietly hum the air of "One More River"*

1.   And when the ark
     Came safe to shore
     God said to Noah and his crew.
     Open the hatches,
     Free the animals,
     Get digging organised,
     The seeds planted,
     For we are starting
     All over again.

C.   HYMN. Come ye thankful people, come *or* SONG. Lord of the Harvest. (*Faith, Folk & Festivity*)

1.   O all ye producers of food, bless ye the Lord
2.   O all ye butchers and bakers, bless ye the Lord
3.   O all ye roundsmen and milkmen, bless ye the Lord
1.   O all ye canners and farmers, bless ye the Lord
2.   O all ye managers and shop assistants, bless ye the Lord.
G.   Praise him and magnify him for ever.
1.   Let us turn the supermarket
     Into the church
     And the church into
     The supermarket.
     Let us pull out the pews
     And wheel in the goods.
     Line by line,
     Cage by cage,
     Cold store,
     Deep freeze,
     All living things,
     All edible forms
     From mousse to macaroni.
2.   Let us take the pews
     And the pulpit
     And the choir
     And fit them somehow
     Into the supermarket.
3.   Let us turn
     The market into the church
     And the church into the market,
1.   Moving down the aisles
     With your plastic perambulator,
     Let your eyes wander
     From left to right
     Even if you resist
     The temptation
     To tumble what you see
     Into your personal pram.
     Consider the marshalled products
     Of earth and sea and sky,
     Hygienically packed
     In contemporary wrappings.
     Untouched by human hands,
     Unloved by human hearts.
2.   But the harvests of the earth
     Are here for your choosing.
     Here in the supermarket,

26

In the village store,
Or the little shop on the corner,
Or the allotment patch,
Or in the kitchen garden.
So much for so many
Just move your hand
And all the harvests of the earth
Drop into your basket.

B. Moving down the shelving
On your left and right,
Tea and corn and crumpets
All for your delight.
Fish from foreign oceans,
Fruit from distant lands,
Peaches and bananas,
Oranges and yams.

D. Marmalade and pickles,
Bacon and spiced ham.
Biscuits plain and fancy,
Sandwiches and jam.
Butter from New Zealand,
Cheeses from the dales,
Cockles, whelks and mussels.
Bottled beer and ales.

B. Bread in many guises,
Soft and crispy rolls.
Slimming foods for diet,
Frozen cod and soles,
Sugar from Jamaica,
Oranges from Spain,
Coffee from Mombasa,
Canada for grain.

D. Ships across the ocean
Laded low with food,
Railway and road haulage,
Oil refined and crude.
Mechanised and mighty,
Signs of weal and wealth,
Harvests home and foreign
For your joy and health.

Joyful music which slowly dies away is followed by the beat, beat, beat of a drum in slow time.

3. But before we get too pleased
And satisfied,
It would be well to remember
Another side of the story.
Why spoil Benedicite
To remind us
Of our privilege
Or our affluence?
We who so often complain
Of the hardness of our lot,
Of the high level of taxation,
Of the smallness of profits
And the cost of insurance stamps.
Do we or dare we forget

Millions of our fellows,
Refugees, victims of war,
Children in despair,
Living, if they live at all,
At subsistence level.
Poverty in plenty
And we stand knee deep in plenty.

E. SONG. Pop goes the money. (*Faith, Folk & Festivity*)

B & D. Give us this day
Our meagre ration
Of rice or meal,
Of dried or processed milk.
Just a few calories,
Some of your despised
And unwanted carbohydrates.
Give us this day
What you give to the pigs
Or to your poodles.
Give us this day.
Your rubbish and your waste.
Give us this day
Your mercy and compassion.
A. Give us this day
Sufficient bread
To let our feeble bodies
Move for another day
And rest fretfully
For another night.
1. Let us turn the supermarket
Into the church
And the church
Into the supermarket.
2. Let the mercy and compassion
Of the Lord Christ
Mould us and move us
Now and forever.
1. Benedicite.
2. Bless ye the Lord.
1. Benedicite omnia opera.
G. O all ye works of the Lord
Bless ye the Lord.

The choir sing softly a part of the Benedicite and if the setting is familiar the people join in.

C. THE GENERAL THANKSGIVING.

The gong sounds once.

Congregational Sheet

BENEDICITE (Harvest)

HYMN. To thee, O Lord, our hearts *or* SONG. Creation's Song (*See Note A*)
Benedicite. First Sequence.

HYMN. All creatures of our God and King *or* SONG. Wonderful is thy handiwork. (*See Note A*)
Benedicite. Second Sequence

HYMN. O praise ye the Lord, praise him in the height *or* SONG. Let the cosmos ring. (*See Note A*)
Benedicite. Third Sequence

SONG (sung by the children). One more river
Benedicite. Fourth Sequence

SONG. Pop goes the money (*Jim Stringfellow*)
Benedicite. Final Sequence

BENEDICITE. The congregation join the choir in singing (*part of*) the Canticle

THE GENERAL THANKSGIVING.

Note A. *If it is desired to duplicate copyright words of these songs for use by the congregation, permission can be granted on payment of a fee of* 50p (10/-) *for each song to Galliard Ltd., Queen Anne's Road, Great Yarmouth, Norfolk*

POLLUTE or PERFECT? (Harvest)

In this order, the passage "Good timber this . . . " is from "Son of Man" by Dennis Potter and is printed by permission of Andre Deutsch Ltd. Permission to perform this should be sought from Clive Goodwin Associates, 79 Cromwell Road, London SW7, stating the length of the extract is 350 words. The prayer "Lord, men lost their lives . . ." is printed by permission of the Christian Education Movement. The passage "Lift up your head . . ." is from Pierre Teilhard de Chardin's "le Mileau Divin" and is printed by permission of Collins Publishers. The verse, "God of grace, and God of glory" is by H. E. Fosdick and is printed by permission of his son. The hymn "God of concrete, God of steel" is by Richard Jones © 1968 Galliard Ltd; the tune will be found in Hymns and Songs (Methodist Publishing House). The prayer "Then it is really true, Lord . . . Lord, so be it" is from Pierre Teilhard de Chardin's "Hymn of the Universe" and is reproduced by permission of Collins Publishers. The hymn "Lord, bring the day to pass" is by Ian Fraser © 1969 Galliard Ltd. The tune will be found in New Songs for the Church, Book 1. Psalm 148 (Jerusalem Bible) is printed by permission of Darton, Longman and Todd Limited.

Characters in the script are designated as follow: L. Leader of worship, C. Congregation, CL. Congregation (left side), CR. Congregation (right side), M. Man in first scene, W. Woman in first scene, R. Radio voice in first scene, 1,2,3,4,5,6. Readers.

The script begins with a domestic scene. The floor should be covered with a large sheet of plastic or fabric which can be gathered up quickly with its contents at the end of the sketch. The floor of the room is strewn with newspapers and magazines, obviously discarded. The table is littered with empty cans, bottles and sweet cartons. M and W sit in easy chairs with a coffee table between them. M reads the newspaper and W paints her fingernails as the radio is playing loudly. Both ignore it. The Radio Voice, R, should be pre-recorded on tape.

R. A report has just been published for the United Nations Economic and Social Council on the "Problems of the Human Environment". It says that in the United States of America the atmosphere absorbs 142 million tons of smoke and noxious fumes every year. (*M lights a pipe making great clouds of smoke causing W to cough.*) Of this total, 36 million tons of carbon dioxide are caused by jet aircraft flying over New York City. (*M fills his tobacco pouch from a tin and throws the tin on the floor.*) An estimated 48,000 million cans and metal containers are discarded. (*W realises her nail varnish bottle is empty and throws it on the floor.*) As many as 26,000 million bottles and jars are thrown away and 20 million tons of paper is collected annually. (*M throws down his newspaper and picks up another. W pours out drink from small type bitter lemon bottle and throws the bottle on to the floor.*) The report goes on to suggest ways and means of improving what is described as a problem which is endangering the future of life on earth. (*W picks up a magazine or two, scans them and drops them on to the floor. M eats sweets, throws down empty cartons: W unwraps a chocolate bar and throws down wrappings whilst Radio plays "Pollution" by Tom Lehrer (on Reprise R 6179).*)

W. Just like the Yanks to make a mess of their lives. Couldn't be like it myself, could you, luv?

M. What? Eh? No! Course not (*couple walk off leaving debris*).

SONG. A Cry of Spirits. (*Faith, Folk, & Festivity*)

1. The United Nations report goes on to describe the problem which is endangering the future of life on earth. . . . How 500 million hectares of arable lands have already been lost through erosion and salinization, how 2/3rds of the world's forest areas have been lost to production, how 150 types of birds and animals have become extinct through human agency. How nearly a thousand species of wild animals are now considered to be rare or in danger. How even the penguins of the Antarctic have traces of DDT in their bodies. It's not their problem, it's our problem. The way to avoid increased human misery and mortality is urgent co-operation on a global scale. We take the good things God gave us in order to hurt each other—can that be right?

Lights out as doleful orchestral music is played while stage is cleared and scene is set for Calvary extract from "Son of Man". A solitary bloodstained cross is erected in centre of stage; lights up as the actors enter, all but J = Jesus, move about uneasily. They can wear traditional Eastern peasant costume if available. A = Andrew, Ju = Judas, P = Peter, Jo = John. J goes to the cross. He almost strokes at the wood, his expression interested.

J. Good timber, this. Hewed with the grain from the heart of the tree. I could fill a room with tables and chairs with wood like this. *He chops the air with his hand.* Cha-ow! Split, it would, straight as ever you could want. Yes! There's nothing like a bit of wood in your hands. Cha-ow! Not a knot in it, see? Good stuff. *He puts his head against the cross, as though it were a pillow, and momentarily closes his eyes.* (*Whispers*) Father . . .Father. . . . *His shoulders start to shake, as though in sobbing. A. steps forward anxiously to comfort him, putting his hands on J's shoulders.*

A. Oh, Master, please. . . . *But J turns swiftly, and we see that far from sobbing, he is in fact shaking with laughter.*

Ju. Wh-what is it?

J. (A tree! A t-tut-tree) *He laughs out loud, then speaks, still smiling.* God puts it in the soil. A tiny little seed. He sends the sun to warm it. He sends the rain to feed it. He lets the earth hug the little plant like a mother with a baby. So it grows. Years and years it grows. Little roots like veins twisting underneath our feet. First it's a sapling, tossed by the wind, a feeble thing. But still sun, rain, still it grows. And grows. Oh, a huge thing. A great strong tower climbing towards heaven. Older now than a man, than two men. What has it not seen? Eh?

P. (*child-like*). Go on—go on.

J. Cha-ow! Down it comes! Crash! Oh, great tree, brought low by the axe. Eh? But God doesn't mind.

Ju (*aloof still*). Doesn't he? How do you—?

J. No-oo. What are trees for? Wood. God wants us to build. To have tables to eat off. Chairs to sit on. He has filled the earth with good things, all for man, for me, for you. So He doesn't mind, does He? No-oo. All that sun. All that rain. All those years. All that struggle from seed to giant—well, tables and chairs are fine things too! But look what we do. Look! A cross! To kill a man! All that sun. All that rain. And here is the end of it—something to hold up and stretch out a man while he dies! *Again, he throws his head back and laughs. The others are puzzled and even rather disapproving.*

Jo. But what is funny about that, Lord?

J. Man!

A. What?

J (*angry rhetoric*). Man! That's what is *funny* about it! Man, silly, stupid, murdering man! We take the good things God gave us in order to *hurt* each other!

Darkness, silence as players go off stage, lights up on Cross which remains in situ *for remainder of service.*

1. Can that be right? We take the good things God gave us in order to hurt each other.
L. Let us pray.
    For our poisoning of the air,
    For our pollution of the sea,
    For our prostitution of the land.
    Good Lord.
C. Forgive us.
L. For our erosion of the soil,
    For our wastage of minerals,
    For our distortion of vegetation,
    Good Lord.
C. Forgive us.
L. For our misuse of chemicals,
    For our corruption of the atom,

For our abuse of machines,
Good Lord.
C. Forgive us.
L. For our infection of the healthy,
For our contamination of the weak,
For our extinction of the rare,
Good Lord.
C. Forgive us.
L. For the perversion of our minds,
For the pollution of our lives,
For our poisoning of your world,
Good Lord.
C. Forgive us.

SONG: Loving All in All for **us.** (*Faith, Folk & Festivity*)

2 (*addressed to congregation*). Will you stop all this complaining! If we didn't produce pesticides thousands of acres of healthy crops would be ruined, whole villages would be wiped out by malaria. If we didn't add certain chemicals to river water vegetation, cattle and people would shrivel up in the long searing droughts of the Equator. If we hadn't experimented with a nuclear device we should never have discovered the vast potential of uranium just at a time when the coal faces of the world are diminishing. Let's hear a word for the progress of man. All right—so our countryside is still littered with the remains of worked out mines. Tin in Cornwall, coal in Wales, lead in the Lake District. But still the quest goes on. When one resource fails, God grants another. "Behold I am making all things new". Like God, we're striving for perfection in the world. After all it's the job he gave us. Doesn't the Psalmist say that He made men "a little less than God, crowning him with glory and splendour and made him lord over the works of his hands setting all things under man's feet".

SONG: Wonderful is thy handiwork. (*Faith, Folk & Festivity*)

Bible Reading: Job 28.1–6, 9–11. (*preferably from Jerusalem Bible*)

Alternate verses read by congregation. CL — odd verses, CR — even verses.

L. Let us pray.
Lord, men lost their lives on an oil rig in the North Sea searching for new supplies of gas to provide power and light and warmth for us.
So through the ages man has quarried at the rock face, or penetrated into the bowels of the earth;
harnessing the power of running water for hydro-electric systems, cutting down the timbers of the forest, dependent on wood for furniture and paper making;
searching the beaches of our coast lines for seaweed and other vegetation to make dyes; studying the waves of power in the atmosphere for use in beaming radio and television signals.
Lord, for the enquiring and adventurous and inventive spirit in man, for the mineral resources of the earth in all their abundance,
We give thankfulness and praise.
2. And we keep going until we arrive at the fullness of God's creation and who knows where that will lead us? During the next thirty to forty years, a number of reputable scientists believe that these new discoveries will be developed:
4. The removal of salt from seawater at an economic cost.
5. Economic mining of the sea floor.
6. Ocean-bed farming which will produce at least 20% of the world's food.
4. The creation of primitive artificial life.
5. Breeding intelligent animals to perform simple labour tasks.

32

6. Genetic control of hereditary defects in human beings.
4. The creation of new organs through transplanting.
5. Implanting artificial organs of plastic and electronic material.
6. Biochemicals to stimulate the growth of new organs and limbs.
4. The wide usage of certain drugs to change personality traits.
5. Biochemical immunisation for viral diseases.
6. Chemical control of the ageing process to extend life by 50 years.
4. Direct interaction between the human brain and computers.
5. The use of telepathy and extrasensory perception in communication.
6. A long-duration coma to permit time-travel.
L. Lift up your head. Look at the immense crowds of those who build and those who seek. All over the world, men are toiling—in laboratories, in studios, in deserts, in factories, in the vast social crucible. The ferment that is taking place by their instrumentality in art and science and thought is happening for your sake. Open then your arms and your heart, like Christ your Lord and welcome the waters, the flood and the sap of humanity. Accept it, this sap—or you will wither, and tend it, or, without your sun, it will disperse itself wildly in sterile shoots.
L. Let us pray.
L & C. God of grace and God of glory.
On thy people pour Thy power,
Crown Thine ancient Church's story,
Bring her back to glorious flower.
Grant us wisdom,
Grant us courage,
For the facing of this hour.

HYMN: God of concrete, God of steel,
God of piston and of wheel,
God of pylon and of steam
God of girder and of beam,
God of atom, God of mine,
All the world of power is Thine!

Lord of cable, Lord of rail,
Lord of motorway and mail,
Lord of rocket, Lord of flight,
Lord of soaring satellite,
Lord of lightning's livid line,
All the world of speed is Thine.

Lord of science, Lord of art,
God of map and graph and chart,
Lord of physics and research,
Word of Bible, Faith of Church,
Lord of sequence and design,
All the world of truth is Thine!

God whose glory fills the earth
Gave the universe its birth,
Loosed the Christ with Easter's might,
Saves the world from evil's blight,
Claims mankind by grace divine,
All the world of love is Thine!

3. With all this talk of pollution and perfection, isn't it time someone said something about the purpose of it all? The Bible not only talks of creation, and the way we distort it, but also about where it's all going to end. It talks about a diversity of talents, jobs and

people held together in the unity of Christ.   Grace was given to each of us according to the measure of Christ's gift. And his gifts were that . . .

4.   Some should be apostles.
5.   Some prophets.
6.   Some evangelists.
4.   Some pastors and teachers.
5.   Some scientists and technocrats.
6.   Some nuclear physicists.
4.   Some biochemists and neurologists.
5.   Some computer programmers.
6.   Some astronauts, some agriculturalists.
4.   Some economists, some educationalists.
5.   Some poets, some politicians.
6.   Some salesmen, some housewives.
3.   All for the equipment of the saints, for the work of ministry, for building up the body of Christ until we all attain to the unity of the faith and the knowledge of the Son of God, to mature manhood, to the measure of the stature of the fullness of Christ. But the Bible goes farther than that. It ends with a vision of the end. But first listen to the words of William Blake.
"The last judgement is not fable or allegory, but vision. Vision or imagination is a representation of what eternally exists, really and unchangeably. Fable or allegory is formed by the daughters of memory. Imagination is surrounded by the daughters of inspiration. The Hebrew Bible and the Gospel of Jesus are not allegory, but eternal vision or imagination of all that exists."
5.   The vision of Christ opening up new vistas to those who will live in community with Him:
Revelation 3. 20–22.
6.   The vision of Christ intrinsically bound up with the pollution and perfection of the world:
Colossians 1.15–20.
4.   The vision of Christ majestic in the glory towards which all of creation is progressing:
Revelation 4.1–8a.
4, 5, 6.   Revelation 4.8b.
4.   Revelation 4.9–10.
4, 5, 6.   Revelation 4.11.
L.   Then is it really true, Lord? By helping on the spread of science and freedom I can increase the density of the divine atmosphere, in itself as well as for me, that atmosphere in which it is always my one desire to be immersed.
By laying hold on the earth I enable myself to cling closely to you. May the kingdom of matter, then, under our scrutinies and our manipulations, surrender to us the secrets of its texture, its movements to history.
Lord, so be it.
C.   Lord, so be it.
L.   May the world's energies, mastered by us, bow down before us and accept the yoke of our power.
Lord, so be it.
C.   Lord, so be it.
L.   May the race of men, grown to fuller consciousness and greater strength, become grouped into rich and happy organisms in which life shall be put to better use and bring a hundred-fold return.
Lord, so be it.
C.   Lord, so be it.
L.   May the universe offer to our gaze the symbols and the forms of all harmony and all beauty.
Lord, so be it.
C.   Lord, so be it.

L. I must search, and I must find
    What is at stake, Lord, is the element wherein you will to dwell here on earth.
    What is at stake is your existence amongst us.
    Lord, so be it.
C. Lord, so be it.

The offertory is received and dedicated using the Prayer from Contemporary Prayers for Public Worship, p. 68 No. 10.

Hymn: Lord, bring the day to pass
    when forest, rock and hill,
    the beasts, the birds, the grass,
    will know thy finished will:
    when man attains his destiny
    and nature its lost unity.

    Forgive our careless use
    of water, ore and soil—
    the plenty we abuse
    supplied by other's toil:
    save us from making self our creed,
    turn us towards our brother's need.

    Give us, when we release
    creation's secret powers,
    to harness them for peace
    our children's peace and ours:
    teach us the art of mastering
    which makes life rich and draws death's sting.

    Creation groans, travails,
    futile its present plight,
    bound—till the hour it hails
    the newfound sons of light
    who enter on their true estate.
    Come, Lord: new heavens and earth create.

3. Alleluia!
    Let Heaven praise Yahweh (the Lord).
CL. Praise him, heavenly heights.
CR. Praise him, all his angels.
CL. Praise him, all his armies!
CR. Praise him, sun and moon.
CL. Praise him, shining stars.
CR. Praise him, highest heavens.
CL. And waters above the heavens!
2. Let them all praise the name of Yahweh,
    At whose command they were created;
    He has fixed them in their place for ever,
    by an unalterable statute.
3. Let earth praise Yahweh.
CL. Sea monsters and all the deeps.
CR. Fire and hail, snow and mist.
CL. Gales that obey his decree.
CR. Mountains and hills.
CL. Orchards and forests.
CR. Wild animals and farm animals.
CL. Snakes and birds.
1. All kings on earth and nations
    princes, all rulers in the world.

2. Young men and girls.
3. Old people and children too!
1, 2, 3. Let them all praise the name of Yahweh.
CL. For his name and no other is sublime.
CR. Transcending earth and heaven in majesty.
CR. Raising the fortunes of his people. Amen.

Congregational Sheet

POLLUTE OR PERFECT? (Harvest)

At home
Song by Tom Lehrer: Pollution
A spokesman on Pollution
Song: A cry of spirits (*see Note E*)
Calvary
A prayer for forgiveness. After the words "Good Lord", the congregation respond "Forgive us"
Song: Loving all in all for us (Normal C. Habel) (*see note E*)
A spokesman on Perfection
Song: Wonderful is your handiwork (Sister Oswin) (*see note E*)
Lesson: Job 28.1–6, 9–11, *read alternately by the congregation.* (*Note D*)
A prayer of thanksgiving
Where will it lead us?
Prayer of responsibility, *said by the congregation* (*see note A*)
Hymn: God of concrete, God of steel (*see note B*)
A spokesman on Purpose
Lessons: Ephesians 4.7, 4.11–13, Revelation 3.20–22, Colossians 1.15–20 and Revelation 4.1–11.
A prayer for commitment. *After the words* "Lord, so be it", *the congregation say* "Lord, so be it"
The offertory is received and dedicated.
Hymn: Lord, bring the day to pass (*see note C*)
Psalm 148 (*see note D*)

Note A.   The verse "God of grace and God of glory" may be included in full on the sheet. Permission to duplicate for local use has been given by the late Dr Fosdick's son

Note B.   This contemporary hymn is in many recently published hymnbooks. If you have not a book containing it, you will need to print the hymn in full on the sheet. Permission for this reproduction for use in a local situation can be given on payment of a fee of 50p (10/–) to Galliard Ltd, Queen Anne's Road, Great Yarmouth, Norfolk

Note C.   Unless your congregation have copies of "New Songs for the Church" Book 1, you will need to print the hymn in full on this sheet. Permission for this reproduction for use in a local situation can be given on payment of a fee of 50p (10/–) to Galliard Ltd, Queen Anne's Road, Great Yarmouth, Norfolk

Note D.   These passages, preferably from the Jerusalem Bible, will need to be included on congregational sheet with a note about left and right hand sides. Consent of the appropriate copyright owner will be required

Note E.   If it is wished to sing either of these congregationally, it will be necessary to reproduce the words on the sheet. Permission to do this can be granted on payment of a fee of 50p (10/–) in each instance to Galliard Ltd, Queen Anne's Road, Great Yarmouth, Norfolk

MAN, FELLOW-WORKER WITH GOD (Harvest)

The traditional Harvest Festival appears to contain two distinct elements: thanksgiving for the fact that we have enough to eat, and the offering of our daily work to God. When we were all directly involved in the production of food it was natural that these two should go together. In our modern situation it becomes possible, and perhaps necessary, to separate the two elements. This order of service was first used the Sunday following a service when the main theme was Thanksgiving for all that we enjoy, in which was included concern for those who enjoy a great deal less.

The phrase "Forgiveness does . . ." is from "The old man of the mountains" by Norman Nicholson and is reproduced by permission of Faber and Faber Ltd.

In the script the designations used are: C = Congregation, L = Leader of Worship, 1, 2, 3 = Readers (1 being the youngest and 3 the oldest), A, B, D, E, F, G, H, I, J = Representative speakers of occupation groups referred to in the script.

C. HYMN: Behold us, Lord, a little space
     or SONG: Working Days (*Faith, Folk & Festivity; a piano version may be found in New Songs for the Church Book* 1).

L. Genesis 1.28 (beginning at "God said . . ."), Romans 8.28.

PRAYER OF ADORATION (*from Contemporary Prayers for Public Worship, p. 132 No.* 2).

(*The different sections should be spoken by readers* 1, 2, 3.)

PRAYER OF CONFESSION.
L. God our Father, we remember now the kind of people we are. It is because we were made in your image that we are here; yet we have distorted the image. You made us to be like yourself—loving and creative; too often we have only been distrustful and destructive. When we live up to our true humanity, and work with you in your world, we can think and plan and make and do great things; but we bury our talent in the ground, fearing to use it in case we lose it. Because of our distrustfulness and our timidity, we fail to do good and we often do wrong. So we come now to confess our failure and to ask for forgiveness. Forgive us now, for Jesus' sake.

DECLARATION OF FORGIVENESS
L. When we confess our sin, God is faithful and just to forgive us our sin. We are forgiven. Thanks be to God.

PRAYER OF SUPPLICATION
L. "Forgiveness does not mean escape from consequences but grace to face the consequences." Father, remembering that we have been forgiven, may we return to our daily life and work with new strength to live the life that you have given us, working always for your glory, and for the true glory of man. Through Jesus Christ our Lord. Amen.

C. HYMN. All creatures of our God and King.
     or SONG. Wonderful is your handiwork. (*from Faith, Folk & Festivity*)

1. Genesis 1.1–3 and 1.24–31.
2. Colossians 1.15–20.
3. John 1.1–14.

C. HYMN. Come, Holy Ghost our souls inspire (Veni Creator) *or* SONG. Fire is lighting torch and lamp at night. (*from Faith, Folk & Festivity p.* 20, *a piano version is available in New Songs of the Church Book* 1)

THE SERMON, *which should not be so long as to detract from the importance of what follows.*

C. HYMN. God of concrete, God of steel. (*Richard Jones*) (*The words of this hymn will be found in full on p. 33 of this book*)

Announcements *are then made concerning the local congregation, the wider church, reference being made to prominent events in God's world this weekend.*

PRAYERS FOR THE CHURCH and THE WORLD. 1,2,3 *read material based on Contemporary prayers for Public Worship p. 55, No. 18, sharing the words where appropriate.*

C. Amen.

SONG. You were there (*from Faith, Folk & Festivity*), *the congregation could join in the refrains after each verse.*

THE OFFERING AND DEDICATION OF DAILY WORK

L. We are all now going to offer our daily work to God. Members of the congregation will represent some of the many different kinds of work by which the daily life of the world is carried on. The first group represent all those whose work involves the exploitation of natural resources—taking what already exists in the world and using it for our benefit. Will the members of this group please stand? (*pause*)
Lord God, your world is full of riches: the earth itself, in which we grow our crops; the sea, swarming with fish; the water that satisfies our thirst and generates our electricity; coal and natural gas which give us heat; stone, and timber, and metals with which we build and make.

A. We thank you for these gifts; help us to develop them, and to use them well; and accept our work, Lord God. (*The members of each group remain standing as the others stand to join them*)

L. The second group represent all those whose work involves research into the truth, and the passing on of knowledge. Will members of this group please stand? (*pause*). Lord God, when you made man in your own image, you made him able to invent and plan and discover; and to learn from the experience of others.

B. We thank you for our skill in invention and discovery; help us to develop it, and to use it well; and accept our work, Lord God.

L. The third group represent all those who make things. Will the members of this group please stand? (*pause*). Lord God, when you made man in your own image you made him, like yourself, a maker; and when Jesus lived at Nazareth he earned his living as a carpenter.

D. We thank you for our skill in making; help us to develop it, and to use it well; and accept our work, Lord God.

L. The fourth group represent all those who are servants of the State: Politicians, judges and magistrates, members of the armed forces: the whole army of civil servants. Will the members of this group please stand? (*pause*). Lord God, your word reminds us that the civil authorities are your agents of sound government, working for our good.

E. We thank you for the good order of a just society; help us to cherish it and to extend its influence: and accept our work, Lord God.

L. The fifth group represent all those whose work provides a service, in the home. Will the members of this group please stand? (*pause*). Lord God, all history demonstrates our dependence on each other; when Jesus lived in Galilee and Judea he lived for others, and taught that glory was to be found in service.

F. We thank you for our need of each other, and life together; in our families and in our communities, help us to strengthen it, and to value it; and accept our work, Lord God.

L. The sixth group represent all those whose work provides a service to people in special need: doctors and nurses, social workers and so on. Will the members of this group please stand? (*pause*). Lord God, because you want our willing response, and because we often refuse to give it, the world that you made well is spoilt by needless suffering; we know that such suffering is not your will, and that your gospel is a gospel of healing, proclaimed in word and action by Jesus the healer.

G. We thank you for human compassion and healing skill; help us to develop it, and to use it well; and accept our work, Lord God.

L.   The seventh group represent those who work in transport and communications, that distinctively modern development that brings us physically close to each other by car, train, bus, plane: by letter and by phone; by news printed and broadcast. Will the members of this group please stand? (*pause*). Lord God, you are the Lord of all space and all time; time passes before you in a moment, and space in a single glance; by the discoveries men have made, and by the way we organise our lives together, we are nearer to each other in space and time than we have ever been.

H.   We thank you for our contact with each other; help us to improve it, and to use it well; and accept our work, Lord God.

L.   The eighth group represent all those whose work brings maker and user together, giving the maker his profit and the user the goods he wants—all who buy and sell, insure and finance, in the complex business of commerce and trade. Will the members of this group please stand? (*pause*). Lord God, in buying and selling we distribute the material goods of the world; our world is a market place; and it is only in this market place that our life can be lived and your gospel proclaimed.

H.   We thank you for our many goods, help us to use them well, and to share them justly; and accept our work, Lord God.

L.   The ninth group represents all those who no longer work or have never been able to: the retired, the disabled, those who do not easily fit into our industrial society, those whose worth few recognise, the very old, the very young. Will the members of this group please stand? (*pause*). Lord God, in the body politic there are limbs and organs capable of much activity there are others equally necessary yet rarely appreciated: when one organ suffers, all share the pain; when one rejoices, all are glad.

J.   We thank you for our interdependence, help us to respect and honour each man's worth and accept us for what we are worth, Lord God.

L.   These nine groups cannot have represented all the ongoing work of the world, and there may even have been some present whose work does not easily fit into one of these nine classifications. Now we are to sum up all this offering of work, what has been mentioned and whatever may have not been stated. Will the rest please stand? (*pause*). Lord God, in the world in which we live today we must work to live; and you have given us the natural resources of the world, the skill of human hand and brain, and the continuing inspiration of the Holy Spirit; in the place and in the time in which we live, most of us need to work less than our ancestors and the majority of our contemporaries; and we can enjoy our leisure.

C.   We thank you for skills, for the opportunity to work, and for time to spare; help us to develop what you have given, and to use it well; and accept our life and work, Lord God.

L.   Will you all please sit, Our offering of money will now be made.

(*The offerings are collected; and as they are brought to the Table, the people stand.*) Father accept this offering of money, and use it for the work of your Church; help us to use all our money wisely, through Jesus Christ our Lord, in whose words we pray together, and say

C.   The Lord's Prayer.

C.   HYMN. The fullness of the earth is God's alone *or* SONG. Let the Cosmos ring. (*from Faith, Folk & Festivity*)

L.   Go, serve the Lord in work and in all your living; and the blessing of God go with you all.

C.   Amen.

Congregational Sheet
Man, Fellow-worker with God
Hymn *or* Song (*see Note A*)
Reading: Genesis 1.28, Romans 8.28
Prayer of Adoration
Prayer of Confession

Declaration of Forgiveness
Prayer of Supplication
Hymn *or* Song (*see Note A*)
Reading: Genesis 1.1–3, 24–31
         Colossians 1.15–20
         St. John 1.1–14
Hymn *or* Song (*see Note A*)
The Sermon
Hymn (*see Note B*)
Announcements
Prayers for the Church and the World
Song (*see Note A*)
The Offering and Dedication of Daily Work *during which the varied professions and work of the congregation will be presented. Members of the congregation should stand as the category into which their work fits is mentioned.*
The offering of Money
Prayer of Dedication and the Lord's Prayer
Hymn *or* Song
Prayer of dismissal

Note A. If it is desired to duplicate the copyright words for use by the congregation, the payment of a fee of 50p (10/-) per song should be made to Galliard Ltd, Queen Anne's Road, Great Yarmouth, Norfolk

Note B. This contemporary hymn is in many recently published hymnbooks. If you do not have a book containing it then it must be printed out in full on the sheet, subject to the conditions in Note A

CALLING ALL SAINTS (All Saints Day)

The extract "The purpose of worship . . ." is from "Honest to God" by John A. T. Robinson. Published in the USA, 1963, by the Westminster Press, Philadelphia. © SCM Press Ltd, London 1963. Used by permission. The extract "I simply argue that . . ." is from "Only one way left" by George MacLeod and is reprinted by permission of The Iona Community, Publishing Dept. The extract "On the first occasion . . ." is from "They became Anglicans" the chapter written by John Wren Lewis, edited by Dewi Morgan and is printed by permission of A. R. Mowbray & Co. Ltd. Permission to print the Parody lyrics of the song "Thanks for the memory" has been granted by Famous Chappell Ltd. The following designations are used in this script: 1,2,3,4. Readers, C. Congregation, A,B,C,D etc. AA, BB etc. denote members of the congregation who should be given a copy of the relevant section of the "Prayer of praise for the Saints" prior to the service.

As the congregation assemble, the song "Thanks for the memory" should be played. It is available on records including Decca SPA 38; Ace of Clubs ACL 1261; London America HAR 8134; Columbia SCX 3257.

1. Thanks for the memory
2. Of Andrew and Simon
3. Matthew, Mark, Luke, John
4. Timothy and Barnabas
1. And still the list goes on
    Thank you so much.
2. Thanks for the memory
1. Of Francis and his birds
3. Colomba and his words
4. And miracles and monasteries
    and mysteries we have heard
2. Thank you so much.
3. Many's the time that you feasted
4. And many's the time that you fasted
2. It must have been swell while it lasted
1. You followed the Son,
    Now journey's done.
3. Thanks for the memory
1. Of ninety-five theses
2. Of nuns upon their knees
4. Of sanctity and courage
    And virtues such as these
3. So thank you so much.
4. Thanks for the memory
1. Of the Wesleys, Isaac Watts
2. A Quaker named Fox
3. We Protestants and Catholics
    As well as Orthodox
4. Thank you so much.
1. Thanks for the memory
    But how can we all do
    the self same things as you?
2. How can we all share the same
    Experiences you do?
    We try to so much.
3. We are such ordinary people

But you were as high as a steeple
You're really incredible people
No doubt, no fear
Wish you were here!

4. No thanks for the memory
Of mystic wonderland
That's hard to understand;

1. You might as well come back again
And maybe lend a hand,

2. Awf'ly glad to see you

3. Show us what we ought to do

1,2,3,4. Then we'll thank you so much.

2. Ephesians 2.19–20

3. Hebrews 12.1–2b

4. St. Matthew 5.48

1. The trouble with the saints is that they seem to us to have lived stained glass lives and we only look at them through a glass, darkly; great acts of heroism, quiet moments of meditation, intense devotion, burning zeal, each of them witnesses from a previous age to how they tried to "offer themselves as holy sacrifices acceptable to God". It all seems a bit remote from us, as if they were rather different people who lived abnormally good lives. They never seemed to have to care about normal things, like making ends meet, filling in a set of accounts on time, looking after Grandma or passing "A" levels. Try being a saint when you've got a splitting headache, a list of shopping as long as your arm and a miserable day ahead of you. . . .

SONG. Woman on a bus. (*Faith, Folk & Festivity*)

2. Now that sounds a bit more normal! Yet those people managed to be a bit more saintly than most of us would have been. A bus conductress, a young man, a shop assistant: you can't get a more normal bunch of people than that but there they were, being saintly. How? By being themselves. By being ready to help, to care, to smile and what happened? Someone else's darkness disappeared and not just for the people they helped. A bit of their saintliness rubbed off on someone else who just happened to see what they were doing and appreciate it. Maybe saintliness has got something to do with that as well— appreciating what others do and are. Didn't Jesus say something about "letting your light so shine before men that they may see your good works and glorify your Father, which is in heaven". Look and see the saintliness of others, and listen out for the sounds of the saint amongst the sounds of the everyday.

SONG. Harvey. (*Faith, Folk & Festivity*) (*congregation sing the chorus*)

3. Harvey a saint? What act of self denial did he perform? Where is the long dossier of evidence for his canonisation? If you make a saint of a miner whose only claim to virtue is to be able to listen then you may as well beatify any old Tom, Dick or Harry who is not deaf. What about acts of penance, days of obligation? Is the whole discipline of prayer and faith to count for nothing? Are you going to give no place to worship? What about the holiness of the spirit?

1. The purpose of worship is not to retire from the secular into the department of the religious, let alone escape from "this world" into "the other world" but to open oneself to the meeting of the Christ in the common, to that which has the power to penetrate its superficiality and redeem it from its alienation. . . . The test of worship is how far it makes us more sensitive to "the beyond in our midst" to the Christ in the hungry, the naked, the homeless and the prisoner.

SONG. Where? (*Faith, Folk & Festivity*) (*congregation sing the chorus*)

2. I simply argue that the cross be raised again at the centre of the market place as well as in the steeple of the church. I am recovering the claim that Jesus was not crucified in a

cathedral between two candles but on a cross between two thieves; on the town garbage heap; at a crossroad so cosmopolitan that they had to write his title in Hebrew and in Latin and in Greek . . . at the kind of place where cynics talk smut, and thieves curse and soldiers gamble because that is where he died. And that is where churchmen ought to be, and what churchmen should be about.

4. I can go along this way quite happily but we haven't gone far enough yet. Saintliness is more than hearing the sacred in the secular and responding to it; saintliness has a lot to do with being fulfilled, a complete person. . . . And a complete person is only a complete person as a member of a community—the family, the church, the nation, and finally the family of man. But we shrink from this—we don't want to become human—and so the church, the body of Christ, where we are meant to learn—and to help each other become human is so often the place of death—full stop!—when it ought to be the place where death passes into life. When life comes out of death, then the church is the place which points out and proves Christ's complete care for all men. Then the church, all of us in it, learn the secret of Christ as Man.

SONG. The family of man. (*Faith, Folk & Clarity*)

3. On the first occasion that I encountered a clergyman who actually did assert the humanity of Jesus . . . I was brought up short in my tracks, it was indeed the starting point of my road to becoming a Christian . . . I was forced to make a revaluation of Christianity by the very same mental forces in myself which had hitherto driven me to oppose it. More-over this process of revaluation was not entirely intellectual by any means . . . (there) was the practical demonstration of the creative and "numinous" power inherent in personal relationships which was provided for me by the Anglican clergyman's "charis-matic" leadership of a group of people associated with his church.
    The group was in some ways quite an ordinary group: certainly it did not appear from the outside to be at all "religious" in any sense that I then associated with the word— its members behaved quite naturally and their main common interests were in the dis-cussion of local problems or current national issues rather than in church services. Its focus was not, in the first place, the church at all, but the clergyman's home and the heightened consciousness of personal relationships was caught from the quite striking sense of relationship between this man and his wife—a relationship which was at once close and yet not closed . . . it was only gradually that the rest of us began to realise that this new consciousness of relationship did have something to do with the church—was indeed the outward and visible sign of that special grace of relationship that the Christian community enjoys and passes on from generation to generation as a result of Christ's act of atonement. Once it had begun to dawn on us, however, that what we had encountered was actually an entirely different mode of living in relationship from anything ordinarily known in the world, a redeemed mode of relationship . . . that made the professional "permissive-ness" of the psychotherapist's consulting room seem a pale shadow in comparison, then we began to inquire for more information about the why and wherefore of the church, and especially of that curious ritual action of the church in which the sharing of new life through the mutual bearing of the burden of sins is symbolically expressed by the sharing of the bread and the wine.

4. Saints aren't special people; they are ordinary people in whom the special relationship Christ has with people lives again.

C. SONG. We thank you for the memories. (*Faith, Folk & Festivity*)

1. Let us pray.
    Let us confess our failure to realise our potential as human beings (*pause*)
    Father, hear us
C. Forgive us, good Lord.
2. Let us confess our failure to build new relationships where we work and in our homes (*pause*) Father, hear us
C. Forgive us, good Lord.
3. Let us confess our desire to be less than fully human because it is easier to stay that way (*pause*) Father, hear us.

C. Forgive us, good Lord.
4. Lord Christ who as a helpless baby, received the homage of workmen, the adoration of rulers, the love of a father and mother; instruct us in the way of helpless receiving.
3. Lord Christ who as a young person, grew to maturity through teachers and friends, nature and town; keep us open to those around us who want to come alive by letting us receive from them.
2. Lord Christ who as a man with men, gave with compassion and tenderness, strength and a fire that burnt up the evil within; help us to see the perfection of your relationships.
1. Lord Christ who as the genuine human, free from patterns of dependence and independence; grant us your insights of mutuality; touch us with your grace to free us to be persons; give us the tact and courtesy to deal graciously with all men; to give and receive; to bend the knee and raise the voice in adoration and abasement; whether life exalts or becomes execrable, and at all times of stress and distress learn to receive from your perfect humanity; hidden in your relationship with others; crushed by a cross; where nails liberated you for a risen life into which you incorporate us. (*pause*)
1. Thanks for the memory
2. of silences and tears
3. thirty hidden years
4. acts of love and healing
    which transformed peoples' fears
1. Thank you so much.
2. Thanks for the memory
1. of saying simple things
3. of love and faith,
4. serving our fellow-men
    as if we served our King
2. Thank you so much
4. Many's the time you faltered
    And many's the time you halted
2. But the power of God, it lasted
1. You stood by men
    to the very end
4. So thanks for the memory
    of men throughout the years
    who faced life with a cheer
1. knowing that your life in them
    would calm their every fear
2. (we're) awfully glad to know them
3. Help us now, along with them
1,2,3,4. To thank you so much.

Copyright © 1937 *by Paramount Music Corp. Copyright renewed* 1946 *by Paramount Music Corp. Copyright* © 1970 *by Paramount Music Corp.*

Prayer of Praise for the Saints (*during which the members of the congregation who each have been given an extract of this prayer, offer it from the places where they are kneeling*).

1. Thank you for the memory of those who knew that they were poor; may the Kingdom of Heaven be always theirs
A. John the Baptist, forerunner, prophet, yet much more than a prophet
B. Francis of Assissi, brother to every creature under the sun
C. Ignatius Loyola, prince of paupers, missionary extraordinaire
D. John Bunyan, tinker, poet, prisoner for the Lord's sake
2. Thank you for the memory of those who mourned for the dawning of your Kingdom; may they find consolation
E. Jeremiah, lamenting, suffering prophet of the exile

F. Mary of Magdala whose tears prepared your corpse for a new life
G. Dante Alighieri whose ray of hope transcends the flame of Hell
H. William Blake, visionary, artist longing to possess the infinite
3. Thank you for the memory of those of a gentle spirit; may the earth be their possession
I. Peter Abelard and Eloise, lovers of life, lovers of God
J. Albert Schweitzer, of masterful mind yet serving spirit
K. Simone Weil, waiting on God by waiting on men
L. Good Pope John, humble champion of reform
4. Thanks for the memory of those who hungered and thirsted for what is right; may they be satisfied
M. Patrick, binding to Christ a nation disunited
N. Thomas More, man of conscience, man for all seasons
O. John Wesley, disturbing the peace of the complacent
P. William Booth, General of God's Army
Q. Martin Luther King, dreamer of a world in harmony
R. John and Robert Kennedy, brothers pledged to the brotherhood of men
1. Thanks for the memory of those who showed mercy; may mercy always be shown to them
S. David, Psalmist, who blessed your enemies
T. Stephen, martyr, who forgave your executors
U. Florence Nightingale whose light shone in dark places
V. Gaw Hong, whose sacrifice ended ritual slaughter
2. Thanks for the memory of those whose hearts were pure; may they ever look on God
W. Richard Baxter, preaching as a dying man to dying men
X. George Fox, pulling down the pillars of the world
Y. John Newman, cardinal of great virtue
Z. William Temple, Archbishop, workman for God
3. Thanks for the memory of the peacemakers; may they be glad to be called Sons of God
AA. Abraham Lincoln, dedicated liberator of the enslaved
BB. Mahatma Gandhi, undaunted apostle of non-violence
CC. Dag Hammarskjöld, untiring servant of the nations
DD. Abbe Paul Couturier, inspired father of unity
4. Thanks for the memory of those who suffered persecution for the cause of right; may the Kingdom of Heaven be always theirs
EE. Paul, Peter, apostles, saints, victorious martyrs
FF. Thomas of Canterbury, tradesman's son, Chancellor, Archbishop
GG. Joan of Arc, maid of Orleans, inspiration of armies
HH. Dietrich Bonhoeffer, philosopher, protester, prisoner
II. Thich Quang Duc, Buddhist, burnt by your own hand
JJ. Jan Palach, Czech, burnt for your oppressed land
1. Let us offer a prayer of Commitment. (*the following is said by all*)
C. With all these witnesses to faith around us like a cloud we pledge ourselves, with God's help, to throw off every encumbrance, every sin to which we cling and run with resolution the race we have started. We will never lose sight of Jesus, on whom our faith depends from start to finish; may he lead us on to share the perfection of his saints.

HYMN: For all the saints

1. 1 Thessalonians 3.13

Congregational Sheet

CALLING ALL SAINTS

Sequence. Thanks for the memory
Readings. Ephesians 2.19–20, Hebrews 12.1–2b, St Matthew 5.48
"The trouble with saints . . ."
SONG. Woman on a bus
"That sounds a bit more normal . . ."
SONG. Harvey: *the congregation sing the chorus (see Note B)*

"Harvey a Saint? . . ."
Reading from "Honest to God" by J. A. T. Robinson
SONG. Where? *the congregation sing the chorus (see Note B)*
Reading from "Only one way left" by George MacLeod
"We haven't gone far enough yet . . ."
SONG. The family of man
Reading from "They became Anglicans" extract by J. Wren Lewis
SONG. We thank you for the memories *sung by all (see Note A)*
Prayer of confession: *to the words "Father, hear us" the congregation respond*
"Forgive us, good Lord"
Prayer of healing
Sequence. Thanks for the memory
Prayer of praise for the saints *during which biddings are said by members of the congregation*
Prayer of commitment *said by all (you may type this out from main script without seeking further permission to reproduce copyright material)*
HYMN. For all the saints
Dismissal. 1 Thessalonians 3.13

Note A: If it is desired to duplicate these copyright words for use by the congregation then permission for this can be granted on the payment of 50p (10/-) per song to Galliard Ltd., Queen Anne's Road, Great Yarmouth, Norfolk

Note B: The choruses only of these copyright songs may be duplicated for use by the congregation on payment of a nominal fee of 15p (3/-) to cover both songs. The whole songs may be duplicated on the basis explained in Note A

AH YES, I REMEMBER IT WELL (Remembrance)

This service seeks to take three aspects of Remembrance, childhood, war and the Lord's Supper and to express the reality of Christ's presence and involvement in them. It serves as a prologue for the Communion Service. Careful rehearsal is necessary to ensure the children's parts are presented tidily but without stiffness.

The song "Lord, I love to stamp and shout" is by Ian Fraser (© 1969 Galliard Ltd. published in New Songs for the Church Book 1). The words "Remember, remember . . . poor maiden so" are sung to the traditional air "Early one morning".

Designations used in the script are: L. Leader of Worship, C. Congregation, N. Narrator, A. Children's choir, Q. 1st child, R. 2nd child, S. 3rd child, T. 4th child, preferably a boy, W. 1st adult, X. 2nd adult, P. Clerical voice, U. American voice, J. Japanese voice, M. UK Midland voice, D. UK West country voice, Z. Cockney voice, G1. First German voice, G2. Second German voice, G3. Third German voice, E. Elderly English voice, F. Elderly Eastern voice, Y. Elderly Arabic voice.

Additionally, the characters Jesus, Nicodemus, Judas and another disciple have parts in the dramatised reading from the New Testament. The actors also play rôles in an extract from "The Universal Soldier and his wife" by Peter Ustinov, which is printed by permission of William Heinemann Ltd. and Little, Brown and Company. Permission to perform this extract should be sought from Lawrence Fitch Ltd, 113–117, Wardour Street, London, W1, stating the length of the extract.

Introductory music played before the service begins could include songs like "Ah, yes I remember it well" from "Gigi", "Do, do, do, do, do you remember?" by the Scaffold, "Dearie do you remember when we . . .?" "Try to remember" by Nana Mouskouri from "Over and Over" Fontana LP STL 5511.

1. *"I like youngsters . . . grown ups think they have arrived" from "Prayers of Life" by Michel Quoist.*

As many children as possible enter through all possible doors, converge on central aisle and process towards the altar area singing "Remember, remember the fifth of November, gunpowder, treason and plot" over and over again. When all the children reach the altar area, the chanting dies away and the children sit, crouch or kneel. The narrator enters with the last of the children.

N. Have you forgotten what it's like to be a child? No worries, few responsibilities—only the occasional examination, the threat of facing teacher with unfinished homework, having to admit to Dad that you—and nobody else—broke his electric drill. Do you remember the discoveries you made learning new things about yourself, about machines, new games, fresh ideas?

A. Lord, I love to stamp and shout
testing lungs and muscles out,
other times I curl up still
dreaming till I've had my fill

Lord, I love to watch things fly
whizzing, zooming, flashing by;
engines, aircraft, speedboats, cars,
spacecraft shooting to the stars

Lord, I love to probe and pry
seeking out the reason why
looking inside things and out
finding what they're all about

Lord, I'm many things and one
though my life's not long begun
you alone my secret see
what I am cut out to be

N. Do you remember when you were like that? The sad thing is grown ups do forget too quickly.

Q. Four ducks on a pond, a grass bank beyond
A blue sky in spring, white clouds on the wing
What a little thing to remember for years.

W. (*slowly*). To remember with tears.

X. I remember, I remember the house where I was born.

R. The little window where the sun peeped in at morn.

S. (*singing*). Remember the vows that you made to your Mary
Remember the bow'r where you vowed to be true.

A. (*sing*). Oh; don't deceive me, Oh! never leave me,
How could you use a poor maiden so!

T. (*preferably a boy—shouts*). Don't forget the fruit gums, Mum.

A. Remember, remember the fifth of November
Gunpowder, treason and plot.

N. When Jesus wanted to prove his point about life in God's Kingdom he asked people to remember what it was like to be a child. When Peter, James and John were arguing about who would be Prime Minister, who Secretary of State, who Ambassador in Chief he gave the top position again to a child. When He needed the help of someone—anyone—out of the 5,000 crowd it was a child who gave what he had to offer, and Jesus gladly accepted and transformed it.

The child in us longs for security, simplicity, trust and truth. The adult in us represses our naivety with sophisticated attitudes designed to protect us against the vulnerability of childhood. The adult in us tries to keep the child in us from its utter dependence on others, on parents, on a Father. Modern man has come of age. It must be difficult for him to understand or even remember what it was like to be not only physically but spiritually, a child in arms.

Dramatised reading from St John 3.1–12 (*preferably J. B. Phillips version*) *with three voices representing Narrator (male or female) Jesus and Nicodemus omitting the references to reported speech* i.e. *v. 2 "he began" v. 3 "returned Jesus".*

SONG. Come Love Carolling *by Sydney Carter (Faith, Folk & Nativity. A piano version is available in Songs of Sydney Carter In the Present Tense Book* 1).

A LITANY OF REMEMBRANCE OF CHILDHOOD

L. Jesus said, "Truly I say to you, whoever does not receive the Kingdom of God like a child, shall not enter it". (*pause*) Lord, we remember the joys of childhood, the undemanding decisions, which game to play, which sweet to pick first. We remember the playground squabbles, the tears soon dried, the disappointments soon forgotten.

C. Father, we thank you for our childhood memories. Help us never to forget them.

L. Lord, we recall the attitudes of childhood, an open mind, a trusting spirit, a willing heart. We recall the spiteful gibes, the hurtful blows, the painful silences.

C. Father, let us never outgrow your commendation yet teach us to outstrip your condemnation.

L. Lord, we remember the frustrations of childhood, the mixture of adult and infant, the undiscovered maturity, the yearning to be older, we remember the sanctions, the cautions, the counsel.

C. Father, we thank you that we learnt to live. Help us to live to learn.

L. Lord, we recall the essence of childhood, the acceptance of authority, the readiness of laughter, the humility of innocence. We recall the hopes, the dreams, the ambitions.

C. Father, let us never grow old in your kingdom yet teach us to grow up in love. Amen.

N. When some people remember their childhood they remember Ration Books, blackouts, clothing coupons and the Black Market. Others remember much older songs. "Goodbye Dolly Gray" "Keep the Home Fires Burning" "Over there" "Kiss me goodnight Sergeant Major". They remember a childhood in wartime. Nights spent in Air

Raid shelters. Grandparents on firewatching, Father the man who wrote the letters from France or Germany or Italy. Just how many children have been born into war nobody knows. The child born earlier today in a Saigon back street is just one more in a long line of people who when they remember the noises of childhood, remember the noises of war.

SONG. The Crow on the Cradle (*Faith, Folk & Festivity. A piano accompaniment is available in Songs of Sydney Carter In the Present Tense Book* 3).

P.   At the going down of the sun and in the morning we shall remember them.
C.   We shall remember them.
U.   Remember what they did in Pearl Harbour.
J.   We shall never be able to forget Hiroshima.
M.   Remember the night they bombed Coventry.
D.   Remember Plymouth.
Z.   Remember what they did to dear old London.
G1. We remember what you did to Dresden.
G2. And to Munich.
G3. We cannot forget Berlin.
E.   D'you expect us to forget the trenches at Paschendaele.
F.   We will never forget the 39th Parallel.
Y.   We shall not forget the 6 day war.
P.   At the going down of the sun and in the morning we shall remember them.
C.   We shall remember them.

A LITANY OF WAR

L.   In October 1969 an American author published research on the 54 wars that had occurred since the end of 1945. Let us pray. Lord, we cannot remember when there was no war, we have got used to seeing it around. We are reminded how it brings change, it redresses the population's balance but we forget how it upsets life, it disturbs this generation's peace. Lord, whilst we remember this,
C.   Forgive, before we forget.
L.   Lord, in war nothing remains the same, everything is forced to change. The landscape is potholed, the trees defoliated, the cities are ruined, the churches full. Lord, whilst we remember this,
C.   Forgive, before we forget.
L.   Lord, in war human life is changed, no-one remains the same. Husbands become soldiers, wives become widows, parents become childless, children become orphans. Lord, whilst we remember this,
C.   Forgive, before we forget.
L.   Lord, in war even our language alters, words change their meaning, retaliation is called defence, a weapon, a device, enlist means conscript, engage means kill—or be killed. Lord, whilst we remember this,
C.   Forgive, before we forget.
     Lord, make us instruments of Your peace. When they show hatred, let us show love, when they say "escalate", let us say "conciliate", when they are aggressive, let us be passive, when they create division, let us create union, when they smite one cheek, let us turn the other, when they make war, let us make peace, when they fear the holocaust, let us serve Your Holy Ghost.

SONG. Been on the road so long (*Faith, Folk & Clarity*).

Lights off as strains of Vera Lynn's song "We'll meet again, don't know where" are heard. The actors assume the different rôles for the following extract from "The Universal Soldier and his wife" by Peter Ustinov. This extract can be played without elaborate arrangements for costume or scenery: although the full stage directions are printed here. The speaking parts are: Sergeant, Bugler, General, Rebel, Wife.

"The curtain rises on a stage bare but for a tomb. There are a couple of television cameras, protected by shiny plastic covers against the rain. Soldiers at ease, stand with their backs to the audience. They are wearing camouflage gas-capes. The setting and the costuming are left to the discretion of the director throughout, the only admonition of the author being that the action should be as fluid and theatrical as possible. Any excess of the imagination is an error on the right side."

A new arrival makes his way to the front of the stage. He carries a bugle. A soldier at the end of the line approaches the newcomer purposefully.

SERGEANT: Bugler, you're late.

BUGLER: (*who will later be known as* 35914): Sorry, Sar'nt. See, owing to the rain—

SERGEANT: I don't want to hear no shudderin' excuses. The plungin' facts speak for themselves, got me? You're on a charge.

BUGLER: Yes, Sar'nt.

SERGEANT: Don't you answer back, or I'll make it stiflin' for you!

BUGLER: Sar'nt.

SERGEANT: Now. On the signal bein' given from the television booth up there, you play what?

BUGLER: Last Post.

SERGEANT: Last Post what?

BUGLER: The Last Post.

SERGEANT: The Last Post what? (*Pause; the BUGLER is perplexed.*) Bugler, I am waitin'. The Last Post what?

BUGLER: (*tentative*): The Last Post, Sar'nt?

SERGEANT: That's better. Now, when I raise my right hand in this manner here, you will raise your bugle to what?

BUGLER: My lips, Sar'nt.

SERGEANT: Now we're getting somewhere at last. You will then play the aforesaid piece of music in a manner appropriate to what type of occasion?

BUGLER: Sad occasion, Sar'nt.

SERGEANT: Dodderin' dummit—you don't bleedin' remember, do you? I'll try again. What type of occasion?

BUGLER: Melancholic occasion, Sarn't?

SERGEANT: One more fancy word out of you, and I'll put you under arrest! Do I convey my meanin'?

BUGLER: Yes, Sar'nt.

SERGEANT: As you were, then. We'll try again. What manner of occasion? (*Silence. The SERGEANT shouts.*) A solemn occasion, you half-cock! (*He inclines his head as though tuning a delicate instrument.*) Appropriate to what?

BUGLER: A solemn occasion, Sar'nt.

SERGEANT: What is appropriate to a solemn occasion, then?

BUGLER: The way I play my bugle, Sar'nt.

SERGEANT: The way you play what on your bugle, Bugler?

BUGLER: The Last Post, Sar'nt.

SERGEANT: Got that in yer 'ead, have you?

BUGLER: Yes, Sar'nt.

SERGEANT: You're not very bright, are you?

BUGLER: No, Sar'nt.

SERGEANT: Well, we can't all be bright, can we?

BUGLER: No, Sar'nt.

SERGEANT: That's better. At ease. As you were! At ease. As you were!

(*The GENERAL walks over. The SERGEANT comes to a thunderous attention.*)

Buglar present and correct, sah!

GENERAL: Good. Good. Try and keep the noise down.

SERGEANT: I impressed that on the bugler, sir.

GENERAL (*with a sad, occasional smile*): Good man. You will start playing the Last Post when the Sergeant here gives you the signal. I want you to play it as though you really meant it, as befits a sad occasion.

SERGEANT: And solemn, with your permission, sir.

GENERAL: And solemn. Yes indeed. And solemn. All right, Bugler, on the double!

SERGEANT: Lif right. Lif! Right!

GENERAL: His Grace the Archbishop should be here at any moment. I am told his address to the nation will take about twenty minutes, which is a little longer than I had bargained for. It means we'll have to be right on our toes at the military end—otherwise it'll be a virtual certainty that the programme will overlap into Children's Hour, which follows us at five sharp.

SERGEANT (*shocked*): Good gracious me, sir, if I may make so bold—it's a bit shocking, isn't it? I mean, it's not as though we bury the Unknown Soldier every day, is it? I should have thought it'd do the nippers good to see the ceremony. After all, sir, they'll be doin' their military service soon enough. . . .

GENERAL: Oh certainly, Sergeant, I quite agree. The television boys have been most co-operative, and I'm sure, if the need arises, they'll run us over.

A dishevelled man, the REBEL, has entered, and is surreptitiously passing out pamphlets to the troop.

SERGEANT: Hullo—oh, it's you again, is it? Not content with four years in the fluting brig for desertion, you got to come here of all places with yer filthy coward-like ideas. Get out of it!

REBEL (*laughing*): Still in good voice, Sergeant? That's what I like to hear. Care for a pamphlet?

SERGEANT: Right! Any man takes a bit of paper from this stinking rebel's under arrest, got it?

GENERAL: What seems to be the matter, Sergeant? Oh Lord, another troublemaker.

REBEL: Another troublemaker? The troublemaker! Don't pretend you don't remember me. At Knossos, in the shadow of the blue hills, you had your first taste of me, didn't you? And you reacted as a soldier should. You ran me through . . . from the back. The last words I remember before I died—"Death is too good for this man!"

GENERAL: The last words you remember before you died? Knossos? What the devil are you talking about?

REBEL: You remember. You remember Knossos. The One Hundred and Eighteenth Legion.

GENERAL: (*with a raucous yell—out of character*): AHHHH! Citizens of Rome, witness my triumph!

Guiltily he passes his hand over his forehead.

REBEL: (*in triumph*): You do remember!

SERGEANT: (*fuming*): Christmas, sir, let me get at 'im!

REBEL: Christmas hadn't been thought of yet, but it was imminent. It was imminent.

GENERAL: (*sober, but decided*): Go away, before it's too late.

REBEL: They tell me things have changed—Maximus Severus. They say this is a public park. There's even a rumour this is a free country.

SERGEANT: (*losing his head*): That's right. It's a free country. You're free to come 'ere, and I'm free to spread your guts on the lawn. (*The REBEL lies down.*) What are you lying down for, you dung droppin'? Frightened, are you?

GENERAL: Sar'nt!

REBEL: Passive resistance.

SERGEANT: Suits me. (*He begins kicking the motionless form of the REBEL, shouting.*) It's a free country! I'll show you . . . how free it is . . .

GENERAL: (*not moving*): Sar'nt! Sar'nt!

A pretty little WIFE enters. She is in the last stages of pregnancy.

WIFE: Stop it!

The SERGEANT, who didn't stop for the GENERAL, stops for a woman.

GENERAL: Sergeant! You disobeyed an order!

SERGEANT: (*aghast*): I did? I can't think how it happened, sir. I was provocated. (*His sense of duty wins over his ability to find excuses. He stands stiffly.*) Permission to put myself under arrest, sah!

GENERAL: (*absently*): I'll deal with you later. (*To the wife.*) The public enclosure is over there, madam . . . that is, if you have a green ticket.

WIFE: I don't need a ticket.

GENERAL: I'm afraid you do.

WIFE: I've a perfect right to be here. Whoever heard of a widow being kept away from her husband's funeral?

GENERAL: I don't think you understand, madam. This is the funeral of the Unknown Soldier.

WIFE: I know. That is the exact description of my husband.

GENERAL: But this is the burial of no specific person, madam. It is a symbolic ceremony.

WIFE: There's a body, isn't there? It must have been alive once.

GENERAL: Of course, but it was selected because it was unrecognizable.

WIFE: That's him! I knew it. He was never recognised by anyone—his face, his character, his personality—it was always the same.

N.   Memory has a strange capacity to blur the passage of time so that when we become older the events of childhood become more vivid. The General and the Rebel in Ustinov's play have a timelessness about them which make them the Universal General and the Universal Rebel, one moment facing the hostilities of Ancient Greece or Rome, the next facing the Television cameras on a modern military occasion. It's this capacity to blur time that makes memory such a rich human experience for all men of all time.

Lights off as the melody of a well known Communion hymn is played on organ/piano. The actors form a tableau of the Lord's Supper, seated around table on which is white cloth, a chalice and loaf of bread. When this is ready lights are switched on and the actors mime the events of the Lord's Supper as they are read by 4 voices, Narrator, Jesus (as before), a disciple and Judas from St Matthew 26.19b–31 omitting reference to reported speech. The actors leave stage at the cue "... (they) went out to the Mount of Olives." The chalice and broken bread remain on the table for the remainder of the service.

N.   The nation remembers its dead with a solemnity and a reality of an Armistice Sunday. The Remembrance ceremony for the Christian is here in the fracturing of a loaf and the deep drinking from a cup. In this ceremony, the passage of time is not blurred by memory because who is alive and here who attended that first Lord's Supper? No-one, except that man at the centre of it all, Jesus Christ. We honour his memory through His words by repeating His actions. We remember He is with us and believe His promise to share the lives of those who share his faith. Simply, effectively what started as a memorial feast becomes a celebration meal—celebrating life not death, celebrating reconciliation not enmity, celebrating a return to childhood—the childhood which gives us entry into His Kingdom, "Do this in remembrance of me."

SONG. Let us break bread together (*Faith, Folk & Clarity*)

The service concludes with the celebration of Holy Communion in the fashion normally adopted in the local situation. It is preferable that the chalice and the bread still on the table should be used and that this part of the service be executed without any extraneous material being added. E.g. already the words of institution have been read so that these should not be read again. Should an offertory be collected it can be presented and dedicated with the bread and wine using Contemporary Prayers for Public Worship, P. 71/14 and conclude with the prayer said by the congregation.

C. Remember, O Lord, what thou hast wrought in us and not what we deserve, and as Thou hast called us to Thy service, make us worthy of our calling, through Jesus Christ our Lord. Amen.

Congregational Sheet

AH YES, I REMEMBER IT WELL

Reading. I like youngsters
Children's procession
Narration
Song. Lord, I love to stamp and shout (*see Note A*)
Children's sayings of remembering
Narration
Bible Reading. St John 3.1–12
Song. Come love carolling (*see Note A*)
Litany of Remembrance of childhood (*to be typed in full from main script*)
Narration
Song. The crow on the cradle (*see Note B*)
Adult sayings of remembering
A Litany of War. *The congregation respond to* "Lord, whilst we remember this" *with* "Forgive, before we forget". *The congregation then join in this prayer.*
> Lord, make us instruments of Your peace. When they show hatred, let us show love, when they say "escalate", let us say "conciliate", when they are aggressive, let us be passive, when they create division, let us create union, when they smite one cheek, let us turn the other, when they make war, let us make peace, when they fear the holocaust, let us serve Your Holy Ghost.

Song. Been on the road so long (*see Note B*)
Extract from "The Universal Soldier and His Wife"
Narration
Bible Reading. St Matthew 26.19b–31
Narration
Song. Let us break bread together (*see Note C*)
Celebration of the Lord's Supper
Prayer of remembering

C. Remember, O Lord, what Thou has wrought in us and not what we deserve, and as Thou hast called us to Thy service, make us worthy of our calling, through Jesus Christ our Lord. Amen.